995
FW

To Re ||||||| D0948808 ||||||| Tate

Wit results

Luka-Rose Petcherman

February 6, 1976

THE
SWASTIKA
AND THE
MAPLE LEAF

THE
SWASTIKA
AND THE
MAPLE LEAF
Fascist Movements in Canada in the Thirties

Lita-Rose Betcherman

Fitzhenry & Whiteside
Toronto   Montreal   Winnipeg   Vancouver

© Lita-Rose Betcherman 1975
All rights reserved. The use of any part of
this publication reproduced, transmitted in
any form or by any means, electronic,
mechanical, photocopying, recording, or
otherwise, or stored in a retrieval system,
without the prior consent of the publisher is
an infringement of copyright law.

ISBN 0-88902-022-1

Fitzhenry & Whiteside Limited
150 Lesmill Road,
Don Mills, Ontario.

Printed in Canada

Contents

Acknowledgement is made to the following sources for illustrations appearing in this book:

The National Library of Canada for No. 1 from *Le Goglu,* No. 2 from *Le Patriote,* No. 8 from the *Montreal Daily Star,* No. 7, 9, 10, from the Montreal *Gazette,* No. 12 from *La Presse; Maclean's Magazine* for Nos. 3 to 6; *Le Magazine Maclean* for No. 11.

THE
SWASTIKA
AND THE
MAPLE LEAF

Introduction

Instead of making the world safe for democracy, the Great War of
1914–18 was followed by a widespread disillusionment with democratic government. It did not seem to matter whether a country had
been on the winning or on the losing side. One of the first countries
to opt for dictatorship, to abolish opposition parties, to make a
mockery of the parliamentary system, to smash the unions and to
destroy personal freedom through the uses of terror was the victori-
ous ally, Italy. Indeed, Mussolini's party gave the name to the
phenomenon—fascism. In 1922 the Fascisti made their historic
march on Rome, which ended with King Victor Emmanuel calling
upon Mussolini to form a government. This easy victory fell to him
because fascism appeared to be the only alternative to another phenomenon of the postwar period—communism. This aspect of the
Italian situation also proved the model for all subsequent fascist
movements; fascism fed on the prevalent anti-communism of the
period. The Russian form of authoritarianism was anathema to all
those who felt they had something worth preserving, and proved
unattractive to large sectors of the masses who looked instead to fascist leaders to improve their lot.

In Germany the Depression gave Hitler his opportunity. As
economic stagnation and unemployment spread across the country,
fear of a communist revolution, dormant since the immediate postwar period, revived. But although Hitler exploited anti-communism, his main strategy for winning a mass following was anti-
semitic propaganda. It was not difficult to stir up dislike of the

1

Jews; under the discredited Weimar Republic they had played a prominent part in political and cultural life. In the early thirties Germany found a natural scapegoat for her troubles in her half a million Jews. Fanatical racism was the strongest component in Hitler's make-up and consequently this became the primary factor in German fascism.

Fascism was contagious, and both the German and Italian varieties were widely exported. But Nazism, with its easy-to-imitate anti-semitism, became the pattern for most of the local fascist movements all over the world.

In Canada fascism was a minor but persistent theme throughout the decade of the thirties. Like communism and socialism, it owed its existence to the Depression which hit this country with particular severity. By 1932 the wheat market had collapsed and Canada's total exports—her economic lifeline—were at half their 1929 level. Construction starts were similarly reduced, and stock market prices were in the doldrums, with the fifty leading stocks down over 80 per cent from the halcyon days before the crash. By this time, wage cuts and lay-offs were widespread; the railways alone laid off seventy thousand men and reduced the wages of the survivors. Prices were at rock-bottom; farmers were getting ten cents for a dozen eggs and fifteen cents for a pound of butter ("the lowest prices in memory").[1] But a government campaign to keep up purchasing power could not avail against the facts of life in the Depression. By August 1932, 842,000 men, women and children were receiving relief, handed out by a grudging government: "The individual cannot continue to lean upon his fellow-man forever, and forever turn to the state to correct every misadventure which may befall him," was the unfeeling statement of the cabinet minister responsible for relief grants in the House of Commons.[2] Almost one-fifth of the labour force in Canada was without jobs and seeking work by 1933. There was no unemployment insurance. "It is only recently that it has become possible to recommend it for Canada," remarked a writer in *Maclean's* in the early thirties "without being suspected either of mild insanity or of sinister designs on the economic system of competition and freedom of contract."[3] The Bennett government held firm to a policy of laissez faire long after other countries had abandoned it, and the main remedy his government had to offer the distressed nation in the early years of the Depression was labour camps for the legions of unemployed young men.

In such an atmosphere the "isms" appealed to many. While the number of card-carrying members of either the Canadian Communist Party or the local fascist groups was small, Parlour Pinks and admirers of the dictators were numerous. Disgust with "the system" underlay much of the support for both the Left and the Right; but fascism in Canada, as distinguished from communism, drew its basic strength from a prevalent if largely latent anti-semitism.

In her analysis of the origins of totalitarianism, Hannah Arendt observed that "Hitlerism exercised its strong international and inter-European appeal during the Thirties because racism, although a state doctrine only in Germany, had been a powerful trend in public opinion everywhere."[4] That this was true of Canada is indicated by the fact that a proto-fascist movement, based on anti-semitism, developed in Quebec province even before the advent of Hitler. In the other provinces where local fascist groups sprang up, the soil bed was also anti-semitism; but it lay fallow until encouraged by Hitler's example. To trace the growth of fascism in Canada, it is necessary to begin with the early attempts of Adrien Arcand to organize anti-semitic sentiment among French Canadians.

1 Preconditions of Fascism in Quebec

Of the 156,000 Jews in Canada in 1930, just under 60,000 lived in the province of Quebec. Theirs was the largest and the oldest Jewish community in the country. In the eighteenth century there had been a few Jewish merchants in the major towns along the St. Lawrence, and in the mid-nineteenth century a small influx of English and German Jews had settled there. In the 1880s and 1890s, when pogroms in Russia and Roumania had created a mass exodus of Jews to America, several thousand had emigrated to Montreal and Quebec City. Those who had settled in Canada before the turn of the century were the "old" families. Acculturated but not assimilated, they took their place both in civic life and as leaders of their own community. However, in Quebec as in the other provinces, the bulk of the Jewish population was composed of first-generation immigrants—part of the mass immigration from eastern and central Europe which, in the decades immediately before and after the First World War, vastly increased the population in the older provinces and opened up the West.

Until the 1930s the Quebec Jewish community lived in relative harmony with the French-Canadian majority. Undeniably there was a bedrock of religious anti-semitism taught from the pulpit and in the classroom. There was also a newer brand of anti-semitism for, as the numbers of Jews grew, their habitual occupation as shop-keepers and professionals made them the direct competitors of the French Canadians. This growing competition found expression in the *achat chez nous* movement, a campaign sponsored by small

French-Canadian businessmen to boycott the goods of Jewish producers and sellers. But the ban was never very effective, and prejudice against the Jews was largely offset by good communications in day-to-day dealings since (unlike the English) most Jewish businessmen could speak French. The Jewish minority enjoyed a particularly happy relationship with the long-lived Taschereau government; in fact, two Jewish Liberal members sat in the Legislative Assembly at Quebec City. Perhaps because the French Canadians were so conscious of their own minority status in a country that was three to one English speaking, they prided themselves on their tolerance, the official organ of the Catholic church going so far as to call Quebec "a paradise for minorities."

Then in 1930 a campaign of hate propaganda was launched in Montreal. Three weekly papers—*Le Goglu, Le Miroir* and *Le Chameau*—began publishing the familiar formulations of antisemitism. All three were edited by Adrien Arcand and published by Joseph Ménard. Arcand was a professional journalist, thirty-one years of age. His father had been a labour organizer and his mother was a school teacher and organist. Like most French Canadians, he came from a large family, but there had been sufficient money to give him a good education, first at a classical college and later at McGill for a few semesters in engineering. Ultimately his gift for words had brought him to journalism and he had written for several Quebec papers including the largest daily, *La Presse* of Montreal. The latter had proved a traumatic experience for him. Because he had tried to organize a union among the reporters, the publisher, Pamphile DuTremblay, had fired him and apparently black-balled him in the industry.[1]

He was rescued from this untenable position by Joseph Ménard, the son of a well-established printer and himself a writer of sorts, who wanted to form a folkist, patriotic movement in Quebec. Characteristically, this kind of extreme nationalism was accompanied by a hatred of Jews. Ménard had been casting about trying to put his plan in action, and in the clever, young journalist without a job, he recognized the publicist he needed. Ménard placed his father's printing press at Arcand's disposal, and in August 1929 the first of their papers appeared, *Le Goglu*, a "journal humoristique," which purported to express the views of a nationalistic, anti-capitalist *Quebecois*. Shortly after, they began publishing a Sunday paper, *Le Miroir*, and in March 1930 they added *Le Chameau*.

Ménard may have been a formative influence on Arcand, but it is more likely that the latter brought fully matured opinions along similar lines to the partnership. At any rate, Arcand never deferred to Ménard as his mentor. As he told it, he supplied the ideas while Ménard supplied the means. In an editorial in January 1930, he explained that *Le Goglu* had been started to spread his own idea, which was nothing less than the awakening of a people. He went on to say that since he had only his pen, he could not have done it without his publisher, "a convinced patriot, a genial organizer, the complement at the necessary moment for such an undertaking." They understood each other "without words." Undoubtedly, the partnership was a meeting of minds.[2]

The initial financing of the venture came from a friend of Ménard's, a well-to-do doctor named Lalanne who loaned them $15,000. A further loan of $13,000 came from the owner of an appliance and radio shop.[3] These benefactors were typical of Arcand's and Ménard's supporters, small merchants and professional men who saw in them champions against the department stores, the chains, and above all against their Jewish competitors. Indeed, *Le Goglu* carried advertisements from lawyers, pharmacists, dentists, real estate and insurance dealers, and a variety of tradesmen. In addition, Camillien Houde, mayor of Montreal and leader of the luckless provincial Conservatives, contributed a subsidy,[4] which undoubtedly accounts for *Le Goglu's* violent attacks on the provincial Liberals.

Early issues of *Le Goglu* were devoted to the editor's vendetta against DuTremblay and to a political campaign against the Taschereau government. Arcand's bitterness towards the combined business and government interests was expressed in vicious satirical attacks on individuals. Although his wit was more like a bludgeon than a rapier, it evidently had some appeal because circulation increased rapidly. A month after the paper started, Arcand claimed that DuTremblay, "the big man of St. James Street," had offered him fifty thousand dollars to close it down.[5]

But the settling of old scores was not the reason for the Arcand-Ménard venture. They did not intend to remain merely a publishing operation. They aspired to start a movement in French Canada based on racial nationalism, and in November 1929 they announced the formation of the *Ordre Patriotique des Goglus*. Resembling the patriotic societies which had sprung up in the new nation states of eastern and central Europe, the Order was also in the tradition of twentieth-century French-Canadian nationalism, particularly the brand preached by the ultranationalist Abbé Groulx. The main points of the new order's program were conservation of "our Latin character," purification of society, cleansing of politics, and promotion of the *achat chez nous* movement.[6] Employing a popularized version of these ideas, Arcand set out to rally French Canadians "to again become something in the land of their fathers." By February 1930 he and Ménard were claiming fifty thousand members and, at least on paper, had laid the foundation for a province-wide organization of fifteen zones headed by a Supreme Council of Goglus. The organizational structure obviously derived from Italian fascism. Arcand's admiration for Mussolini created a community of interest with Montreal's twenty-two thousand Italians and gave him one of his most durable constituencies. In the civic elections of 1930, *Le Goglu* urged Italian voters to support its choice of candidate "como boni fascisti."

For the Italian community, fascism was synonomous with nationalism. Most of its members had emigrated from the impoverished south of Italy a generation earlier. In Montreal they were factory workers and labourers and when the Depression came they were very hard hit. Cut off from their neighbours by the language barrier and discrimination, they basked in Mussolini's reflected glory. "This is the first time the colony has had any prestige," one Montreal Italian told Charles Bayley, who wrote a master's thesis on the Montreal Italian community in 1935. Bayley estimated that 90 per cent of the Italians in Montreal supported the fascist movement. Aside from national pride, they were under constant pressure from the Italian consuls general, who assumed the direction of the community. All organizational life was fascist; most noticeable were the Fascisti who donned black shirts for ceremonial occasions. But all cultural organizations, veterans and youth groups, Italian language newspapers, and community centres (the *Case d'Italia*) were directed and subsidized by the Italian government. There were free trips to Italy for the children to indoctrinate them with the fascist ideology, and language schools with fascist teachers. A further pro-fascist influence on the Italian community was the Catholic church. The priests, almost all of whom were Italian-born, urged their flock to support Mussolini in word and deed. An enormous fresco of Il Duce in the church of the Madonna della Difesa graphically testifies to the near veneration in which he was held.[7]

In fact Mussolini was generally admired in French Canada, partly for his strong leadership but mainly because he was supported by the papacy.[8] European liberalism and parliamentary democracy had been marked by a strong anti-clericalism and Pius XI, who came to the papal throne in 1922, regarded liberal ideas as inimical to the church. When Mussolini came to power, this pope found that he got along far better with the Italian dictator than his predecessors had with the various liberal governments since the Risorgimento and, in 1929, the Vatican signed a concordat with the Italian fascist state. As a result, the good Catholics of Quebec, lay as well as cleric, regarded Mussolini in a most favourable light.

In the winter of 1929–30, the Order of Goglus began holding mass meetings, first in Montreal and then in Quebec City where Arcand's lieutenant was the youthful son of a prominent family.[9] In his typically heavy-handed "Goglu" style, Arcand described the consternation in the halls of the Legislative Assembly when word of the meeting and of the young man's involvement became known. In the same exaggerated mode, he depicted the startled faces when he and Ménard appeared one day in the visitors' gallery of the Assembly. The debate happened to concern the admission of women to the bar and prompted Arcand to register his opinion that for women "the glory of the hearth and sublime maternity" were all-sufficing. Although his rejection of female equality was shared by church and state in Quebec, which alone among the provinces stood out against female suffrage, it was also consistent with his other anti-democratic views which now came to the surface.

Initially, only traces of anti-semitism were noticeable in Arcand's writing, although his brand of nationalism was decidedly racist. But after a few months, lead articles and editorials against the Jews began appearing with regularity. The ostensible cause was the Jewish School Commission bill introduced by the Provincial Secretary, Athanase David, in April 1930, and passed into law almost immediately. The legislation's purpose was to set up a Jewish committee to deal with the Protestant and Catholic school boards regarding the education of Jewish children; it did not alter the inferior position of Jewish parents who could neither vote for school board members nor stand for election. From the beginning, this law met with outspoken opposition from the Conservative party and the episcopate, neither of which wanted to see a separate Jewish School Commission, even one with such limited powers.[10] . Thus the atmosphere was propitious for stirring up feelings against the province's Jews. The introduction of the David bill marked the commencement of Arcand's life-long anti-semitic campaign which was to bedevil the Jewish citizens of Quebec and, later in the decade, those of the entire country.

Arcand made the school issue the departure point for an assault on the legal status of Canadian Jews, whom he wished to see deprived of the rights of a minority in a democratic society. It should be remembered that minority rights were a sacred cow in the interwar years, guaranteed by the League of Nations and accorded lip service by all countries. Since French Canadians in particular clung tenaciously to the concept of minority rights in order to stay afloat in a predominantly English Canada, Arcand's solution was to refuse to recognize the Jews as a *bona fide* minority. He maintained that there were only two minorities in Canada—the English in Quebec and the French in the rest of the country. By alleging that Jews were not entitled to minority status—a stock-in-trade argument with all ultranationalist Quebec groups—Arcand was able to refute Jewish claims for equal treatment under the law. The purpose behind the Order became apparent when all Goglus were urged to write their MLA's protesting the passage of the David bill.[11]

Although *Le Miroir* and *Le Goglu* supported Houde in the civic elections of March 1930, Arcand and the volatile mayor severed their connection at this time. Shortly after his re-election, Houde released a statement to the press condemning Arcand's anti-semitic campaign in the strongest terms.[12] Strange to say, at the very moment that the provincial Conservative leader officially disassociated himself from the Arcand-Ménard papers, they became organs of the federal Conservative party.

In the spring of 1930 a federal election was in the offing and both parties were organizing their campaigns. Conservative papers were few in number in Quebec and lacked influence in comparison with the Liberal press. As early as December 1929 R. B. Bennett, the national Conservative leader, had been advised by his St. James

Street supporters that "the local press situation should receive initial encouragement from headquarters."[13] As a result of this high-level assessment, Joseph Rainville, the Conservatives' provincial organizer, approached Arcand and Ménard. In the name of the party he promised them a financial guarantee of $25,000 and further support as necessary, on condition that the Goglus could help the party gain more than twelve seats in the upcoming election.[14] No offer could have been more welcome, since Arcand and Ménard were running heavily in debt.

Rainville's first step was to approach a number of friends to contribute one hundred dollars each towards the up-keep of *Le Miroir*.[15] It is also probable that *Le Chameau*, which began publishing on March 14, 1930, was inaugurated with Conservative funds. The Conservative subsidy became effective early in May when *Le Goglu* announced to its readers that "the views of Mr. Bennett exactly accord with the economic program of the Order of Goglus."[16] Sometime that month Arcand and Ménard met with Bennett and outlined their "plan of procedure and propaganda,"[17] and until the election they campaigned vigorously for him through their papers and their public meetings. In addition, they printed a hundred thousand election circulars. Assisted by the electorate's desire for change in a time of Depression, Bennett won a smashing victory on July 28, 1930, taking an unexpected twenty-four seats in Quebec. All in all, Arcand and Ménard received $18,000 from Rainville for their services.[18]

But a propaganda campaign is expensive and their work for the Conservatives merely compounded their indebtedness. In a memo to Bennett dated January 14, 1931, they claimed that, notwithstanding Rainville's subsidy, they had gone into debt to the amount of almost $50,000, and reminded the prime minister that they had been promised compensation for expenses incurred in the federal campaign. Among the Bennett Papers is a file of letters from Arcand and Ménard beseeching "our chief" for help. Bennett granted them an interview but apparently did not authorize the payment of their debts. During the next year and a half they made repeated trips to Ottawa, always to find the prime minister too busy to see them. While they felt that the party had treated them "like dirty dogs," they did not hold it against Bennett personally. On January 2, 1932, they wrote him that they were proud to serve "the

God-sent man who leads our country so wisely in this hour of great distress and who has all our admiration and confidence."[19] Still Bennett turned a cold shoulder towards them and while they continued to receive a subsidy from the Conservative party, it was sporadic and far from adequate. As one of their friends in the Senate told Bennett's secretary, "Scant help as is given from time to time just prevents starvation, and drags him [Arcand] and his friends to despair."[20] Nevertheless the small subsidies added up and in 1936 a Conservative organizer estimated that the party had spent $27,000 on *Le Goglu* and its affiliates.[21]

It would appear that Bennett had little further use for Arcand and Ménard after the 1930 election. Meanwhile, their anti-semitic campaign had gained momentum during the election campaign. The transformation of *Le Goglu* from a "journal humoristique" into an organ of hate propaganda can be measured by the change in style of its political cartoons. Where previously Jewish politicians were caricatured in the same manner as others, now they were depicted in loathsome stereotypes of the kind associated with Julius Streicher's *Der Sturmer*. The public meetings of the Order of Goglus also openly promoted hatred of Jews, and Arcand's speeches were nothing more than harangues on "the Jewish problem." At a mass meeting in November 1930 at the Monument National in Montreal, his audience was told that Jews isolated themselves, were materialistic, controlled the means of communication including the film industry, regarded themselves as the chosen people, promoted such "evil" ideas as internationalism and liberalism, and were the cause of the Bolshevik Revolution. (Ménard contributed lasciviousnous to the list.) Ominously Arcand remarked that "until now Jews have had a particularly happy fate in Quebec."[22] This was a reference to the fact that the unpopular Jewish School Commission Act was soon to be repealed. In doing so, Taschereau was bowing before the displeasure of the bishops; but the fate of the legislation did no harm to Arcand's prestige. Editorializing on the repeal he called it "a triumph for the Goglus," and he and Ménard took credit for winning the battle against the David bill.

By 1932 Arcand was in touch with fascist and ultranationalist organizations all over the world—"enlightened patriots" he called them—and his writing and speaking reflect their anti-democratic bias. Whereas a few months earlier only the Liberal party had been the object of his criticism, now the party system itself was deemed pernicious. (Some of this, of course, was doubtless due to disenchantment with the Conservatives.) Authoritarian doctrines and a worship of violence made an increasing appearance in the pages of *Le Goglu* and *Le Miroir*.

Arcand was even receiving money from some of these foreign friends. One whom he later identified was Lord Sydenham of Coombe, author of a standard text on anti-semitism entitled *The Jewish World Problem*.[23] Lord Sydenham belonged to the ultra right wing of the British Conservative party. Typical of his enmity towards the Jewish people was the fight he had waged in the House of Lords against the Balfour Declaration establishing a Jewish national home in Palestine. Sydenham was closely connected with British fascists; in fact his book on the Jews was published by a fascist group called the Britons. Like the better known Imperial Fascist League, the Britons was essentially a publishing venture specializing in anti-semitic propaganda. Arcand was in contact with both groups very early. He reprinted their material in his papers and it is likely that they provided the link with Sydenham and other anti-semites among the British Tories. Arcand explicitly stated that the Imperial Fascists were tied in with the traditional Conservative party in England. In any event, there is no reason to doubt his statement that Sydenham and a few like-minded peers lent financial support to *Le Goglu*.

Under the tutelage of the "enlightened patriots," Arcand's anti-semitism became fanatical. His papers began carrying vicious articles like Alfred Rosenberg's 1920 libel on the Jewish race. Sent to Arcand by the Imperial Fascist League, it appeared in *Le Miroir* on January 3, 1932, accompanied by gargoyle-like caricatures of long-forgotten figures such as the anarchist, Alexander Berkmann. Under the headline, "The Drinkers of Blood," old calumny was presented as "sensational" news. Credulous readers were asked to believe that "Israelites had butchered 40,000 Christians in less than five years in Russia." The article asked, "What would Jewish domination be if it could spread into all countries?" and answered, "Barbarity exceeding the cannibals."

The effect of articles like "The Drinkers of Blood" on a parochial readership cannot be over-estimated. Intellectuals did not read *Le Goglu* or *Le Miroir*. When a judge of the Quebec Superior

Court expressed surprise that people could believe such nonsense, an eminent Jewish barrister replied that he would not worry if only the intelligentsia read those papers but their readers were far from that.[24] Unfortunately, the *Québécois* were predisposed by their religious teaching to believe tales of Jewish wickedness. A French Canadian wrote to Mackenzie King in 1938 that "without the Jewish argument Arcand will get nowhere in Quebec. French Canadians are educated in their early childhood to hate the Jews."[25]

So virulent was Arcand's anti-semitic campaign that the two Jewish members of the provincial legislature introduced a group libel bill in the 1932 session. Both Peter Bercovitch and Joseph Cohen were lawyers and therefore familiar with the difficulties involved. Group libel legislation was particularly suspect in the English-speaking countries with their tradition of individual liberty. In the interwar period Canadians placed their faith in the unrestricted freedom of the individual and French-Canadian leaders invoked the famous British freedoms as often as their Anglo-Saxon counterparts. Paradoxically, this insistence on personal liberty for all militated against any semblance of equality. Hate-mongering was allowed in the name of freedom of speech and any attempt to curb the discriminatory practices of a landlord or a resort owner was rejected as an infringement on the rights of the individual. Liberty, as understood in the thirties, necessarily led to the triumph of the stronger; it was Social Darwinism sugar-coated.

Reflecting this laissez-faire liberalism, Canadian law offered no means of redress for a member of a defamed racial or religious group. Libel was an offence under the Criminal Code, but unless a specific person was vilified the Code was of no help. Many years before, S. W. Jacobs, an outstanding Jewish lawyer who had gone on to become an M.P., had fought a successful slander suit against the perpetrators of an attack on the Jews of Quebec City. But a favourable decision in the *Ortenberg* v. *Plamondon* case, which dragged through the courts for years, was ultimately won only because the Quebec Jewish community was small enough to claim that each member was personally affected by the slander.[26] This case, therefore, did not set a precedent for protecting a group from the evils of hate propaganda. Because there was no adequate federal legislation, Bercovitch and Cohen hoped to find a cure through a provincial statute.

On January 27, 1932, Bercovitch rose in the Legislative Assembly and proposed "a law concerning the publication and distribution of outrageous subject matter against any religious sect, creed, class, denomination, race or nationality." Born in Montreal in 1879, Bercovitch spoke French fluently, and was a veteran member of the House. Specifically, his bill provided that any person who believed his group had been slandered could seek an injunction before the Quebec Superior Court. Moreover, without any deposit or guarantee, he could obtain an interim injunction against the person allegedly committing the libel. It was strong legislation, offering broad coverage and immediate relief. The bill was seconded by Joseph Cohen and supported by Dr. Anatole Plante, who represented a riding with a heavy Jewish vote. The rest of the Liberal members were far from enthusiastic, but Premier Taschereau wanted to oblige his Jewish supporters as long as the legislation was not too unpalatable in the province.[27]

Press reaction was predictably hostile. Although it was well known that the Arcand journals were the target aimed at, virtually all the provincial newspapers were incensed at what they labelled an assault on the freedom of the press. The nationalist *Le Devoir* in a sarcastic column by "G. P." (Georges Pelletier, soon to succeed Henri Bourassa as director) regretted that:

> Some people lack all sense of measure, like the sponsors of the bill on outrageous subject matter. Does John Bull get upset when he reads in a Quebec paper that Napoleon called England a nation of shopkeepers? Or Jacques Bonhomme when he reads in a Montreal daily that the French are a race of frog eaters? Or does Sandy become angry at the Scotch jokes in the *Gazette*, or Pat when he reads a story about Irish drinking habits in the *Star*? But is Isaac angry when *La Patrie* writes that the Jews have been and continue to be bankers exacting high interest from everyone and that they have a penchant for usury? Quick, to the nearest lawyer. There the vexed man will demand an injunction against the paper and he will get it.[28]

And the *Montreal Gazette*, notwithstanding its Jewish editor Abel Vineberg, commented that to go to such an extreme measure as the proposed bill was like mounting a huge steam-driven crusher to destroy little kernels of fanaticism. *Le Devoir's* criticism became progressively more bitter, with racist undertones showing through. "This heavy and awkward machinery [referring to the injunction] does not get to the law breaker until long after the violation. As an example, if Mr. Abel Vineberg, editor of the *Gazette*, publishes a libel against the Jewish race, it will be consumed with the breakfast rolls before the law catches up with it." To make the law work, *Le Devoir* continued, there would have to be a censor in each printing shop, appointed of course by Bercovitch and Cohen, "like the kosher butcher shops whence nothing goes out which is not approved according to talmudic prescriptions."[29] This was followed by some slurs on the alleged electoral practices of the two Jewish politicians, and by the inevitable link-up between Judaism and communism.

Other papers followed *Le Devoir's* lead in condemning the bill. *L'Action Catholique* pronounced that "the Province of Quebec, a paradise for minorities, does not merit the affront of a law which would give her the appearance of being more of a persecutor than her sister provinces."[30] The church spokesman went on to say that there was nothing like this law in the United States, France, England or other civilized countries, and asked why Quebec had to be the exception. The press was unanimous that, in order to stop an anti-semitic campaign in a couple of yellow journals, the legislation would cause trouble for all the papers. They were also in agreement that such a law would aggravate racial quarrels and obtain the opposite to what Bercovitch and Cohen sought.

Arcand was in good company. The Bercovitch bill had changed a formerly neutral press to one highly critical of the Jewish politicians, if not of the whole Jewish community. Arcand's own response to the legislation, which he acknowledged was aimed at him, was a hysterical outburst.

The Deputy Beder [sic] Bercovitch, false prince of the filthy ghettos, wants to convert the machinery of our beautiful Catholic and French-Canadian laws to the use and caprice of imported Jewry. In fact, this flotsam and jetsam of the Red Sea, this fugitive from the massacres of Egypt, this leftover from the justifiable furnaces of Nebuchadnezzar, this illustrious descendant of the assassins of Christ, has the characteristic cheek of rats and Jews to ask the parliament of our race for a law which would permit the residue of Yiddish immigrants from Poland and Russia to hinder the rightful claims of an honest and upright race which does not want to submit any longer to the exploitation, thievery, perfidy, immorality, filth, corruption and bolshevik propaganda of the sons of Judas.[31]

The Taschereau government was growing timid with advancing age and took alarm at the bad press. Bercovitch was now under pressure from his own party to retire his bill. While refusing to abandon it, he agreed to make substantial changes, and on February 9 reintroduced it in the Assembly. The revised legislation covered group libel on the grounds of race, religion and nationality only: class, sect and the rest were dropped. In addition, the interim injunction was no longer mandatory, and the matter of a deposit was placed at the discretion of the judge. Outside the chamber, Bercovitch assured the newspapers that he did not want to cause problems for them; he just wanted to impede systematic racist campaigns.[32]

But the papers could not be mollified. With *Le Devoir* in the lead, they stepped up their alarmist offensive. As Georges Pelletier remarked, "Bercovitch has released a rabbit and all the press of the province are giving chase."[33] Since the revised bill answered the main criticisms, the papers sought to find new objections. They now took the position that existing legislation, such as the Civil Code and the Press Act of 1929, was sufficient to take care of the problem. From this followed the argument that Jews were asking for special laws above and beyond everybody else. The facts had become so twisted that *Le Progrès du Saguenay* actually wrote: "There is no need to sabotage the Press Act to the benefit of a fistful of malcontents. The laws common to the province and satisfying to its population ought to suffice for the Jews."[34] That a minority might require special protection was not acknowledged. In this climate of opinion, even the powerful voice of the government's supporter, *La Presse,* was muted, and its dutiful assurance that the bill was expected to pass sounded strangely faint-hearted.[35]

It was not until the last days of the session that the anti-defamation bill came up for debate. Bercovitch began by stressing the tradition of equal rights in Quebec and the justice that all enjoyed regardless of race or religion. He told how this peaceful way of life was being threatened by a few slander sheets whose aim was to sow dissension and turn the people of Quebec against the Jewish people. Where minorities were numerous as they were in Canada, he said, there was a need for legislation to protect any and all races against libel. In concluding his argument he cited the League of Nations resolution on the protection of minorities.

In seconding the bill, Joseph Cohen appealed to French-Canadian pride by reminding his listeners that their 1832 law, permitting a Jew to sit in the Legislative Assembly, was a quarter of a century ahead of Great Britain. That historic legislation, he said, had been proposed by Joseph Papineau, and now his descendants were being called upon to protect Jewish rights once more. It was perhaps unfortunate that Cohen felt he had to refute all the myths of anti-semitism from ritual murder to the "Protocols of the Elders of Zion." It was neither the time nor the place. More to the point was his citation of the judgment in the *Ortenberg* v. *Plamondon* case that group libel did not qualify as defamation. As a lawyer himself, he assured the members that there was no recourse under existing law.

But the Liberals had been effectively warned off by the press, and were not going to support their colleagues' measure. One of their few non-French members, R. F. Stockwell, was chosen to speak against the bill. To add to the drama, it was an open secret that Stockwell and Bercovitch were rivals for the post of Provincial Treasurer. Stockwell took the position that the Jews of Quebec had all the rights of British subjects, including the right to hold property and the right to practise their own religion. He maintained that they were now asking for an additional right—immunity from criticism, and this he would not accord to any race. His next point was a jurisdictional one, namely that the bill created a new crime and therefore was a federal matter. For good measure, he added that the offending journals were unimportant and should be disregarded. In his peroration, he summed up the conventional wisdom: "Let us recall that what is good will survive and what is bad will die."[36] Darwinism, as applied to the field of morals and ethics, was thin armour with which to enter the fascist era. On the one hand it provided liberalism with weak defences in the face of totalitarian success; on the other, it led many basically decent people to believe that whatever happened was necessarily right.

The debate on the bill was continued two days later. Displaying the "exquisite urbanity" which even the unfriendly *Le Devoir* conceded to him, Bercovitch wondered aloud if Stockwell had read the bill. Had he done so, he would have seen perfectly clearly that it did not hinder honest criticism but simply prohibited libel. The Jewish people were only asking for the machinery to assure their reputation and honour. If a newspaper could show that the libel was well founded, no injunction would be granted.

At last Premier Taschereau took the floor. He began by saying that this was one of the most difficult situations he had faced in a long career. He complimented the sponsors of the bill and through them assured the Jewish community that its members still enjoyed the respect of their fellow citizens. He understood the suffering of the Jews at these unwarranted, slanderous attacks because for a year he himself had been the victim of those papers. But he had ignored them and he advised the Jews to do the same. His speech left no doubt that he strongly deplored the anti-semitic campaign, which he described as "anti-national and anti-Quebec." He called it a disgrace in a province which "prides itself on being the refuge of liberty and tolerance, of harmony among races."

However, he told the House that he could not vote for the Bercovitch bill because he no longer believed that "public opinion is ready to accept such a radical measure." Moreover, in his judgment, existing laws were sufficient to protect the rights of minorities. Having decided to take no legislative action for the time being, he fell back on an urgent appeal to the papers in question to stop their attack on the Jewish people. He asked the editors to devote their talent and energy to a better cause and suggested that they strive for the preservation of French-Canadian traditions. Taschereau was obviously playing to the gallery; he was hardly naive enough to think that Arcand would voluntarily relinquish his anti-semitism. To get rid of the troublesome bill, a government member moved an amendment which referred it to a special committee. Since the Legislative Assembly was about to be prorogued, this was tantamount to killing the bill. The vote was 53 to 3 in favour of the amendment.[37]

Arcand was triumphant. The morning of the final debate, he and Ménard had sent a memorandum to each MLA denouncing Jews and Judaism in extreme terms.[38] While this should have pointed up the dangers represented by these fanatical anti-semites, it either had the opposite effect or no effect at all. Arcand could only assume that he had intimidated the legislators. When the next issue of *Le Miroir* appeared, it carried a signed article by the editor and the publisher rejecting the premier's appeal to stop their campaign against the Jews.

II The Hitler Years Begin

In March 1932 Adolf Hitler ran for president of Germany against
von Hindenburg. The day before the election, *Le Miroir* carried his
picture and an article burning with hero worship. If Hitler is
elected, readers were told,

> tomorrow will be the most important date in contemporary
> history. For the first time in modern history a government will
> officially ostracize the Jews, crush their power, and sound the
> rallying call of the Christian political front in the world. [1]

Although Hitler did not win the election, it was obvious that he was
shaping up as Germany's strong man. Canadian newspapers were
full of him, but only *Le Miroir* and *Le Goglu* were wildly enthusiastic,
running headlines such as "Bravo Hitler."

"We have never hidden the fact that all our sympathies belong
to the Hitler movement," Arcand wrote on May 1, 1932. He por-
trayed the Nazi leader as "the champion of Christianity"—possibly
in all sincerity, since at this stage Hitler was playing down his anti-
religious animus. For Hitler, the only religion was Nazism; but for
Arcand's readers, the Nazis were represented as virtually a Catholic
party. Other French-Canadian editors were not so gullible. *Le
Devoir's* coverage of the German elections in 1932 was unfavourable
to the Nazis, recognizing them as anti-Catholic. Arcand, however,
had found his role model and Hitler could do no wrong. The May
1 editorial in *Le Miroir* declared:

> Hitler's policy can be summed up as follows: reestablishment

of Germany's prewar prestige; territorial expansion; annulment of war debt and the Treaty of Versailles; exposure of the public utility trusts; the crushing of Bolshevism and Marxism; disenfranchisement of the Jews, with seizure of their goods (since they stole them from the Germans); breaking up the international Jewish banks; supremacy of the Aryan-Christian civilization.

Thus Arcand was a publicist for Hitler even before the latter came to power.

The rise of Hitler and what Arcand regarded as his own victory over the Bercovitch bill combined to push his anti-semitism to new heights. It had reached the stage of ideology, where the myth of the Jews as world destroyers is seen as the key to history. This kind of anti-semitism is unrelated to reality, has nothing to do with economic reasons or with alleged Jewish exclusivity: it is built on the fantasy that there exists a Jewish conspiracy to which all Jews belong and whose objective is world domination. Psychologically, the ground for this myth formulation was laid by the anti-Jewish demonology of medieval Christianity which fostered the popular belief that Jews killed Christian children and poisoned drinking wells. These harmful stories, which circulated among illiterate people for centuries, probably originated in the fears of early Christians that the parent religion might yet triumph. The idea of the Jewish world conspiracy, however, appears to date from the period following the French Revolution. One of the earliest manifestations is to be found in the writings of an emigré priest who explained the revolution as the nefarious work of a conspiracy of freemasons manipulated by Jews. Because revolutionary egalitarianism led to Jewish emancipation (among other things), it is easy to see how the two ideas of revolution and Judaism became associated. To blame the Jews for the revolution was an easy step for an embittered survivor of the Old Regime. During the nineteenth century the idea of a Jewish conspiracy was kept alive by the clerical Right who ascribed rising secularism and, later, socialism to it. By the end of the century it was the refuge of reactionaries to attribute all that seemed wrong with modern civilization to Jewish world destroyers.[2]

The so-called "Protocols of the Elders of Zion" are the codification of anti-semitic mythology. Supposedly the secret plans of a Jewish international organization for world domination, the Protocols were a forgery concocted by Tsarist police to discredit the revolutionary underground through its Jewish members. The forged document had little influence until the Russian Revolution when it was used as anti-bolshevist propaganda. Some White Russians carried copies with them when they dispersed to various world capitals. In this way the Protocols spread throughout Europe and America. Despite repeated exposure as a forgery, they were used by fanatical anti-semites as "proof" that the Jews were the enemy of the Christian people. This was the rationale which enabled Arcand and Ménard to exalt their defamation of the Jews as "a campaign of national defence." The myth of a Jewish world conspiracy served them as a warrant for slander of the basest kind. So divorced from reality were their charges that, in the summer of 1932, they even accused Jews of murdering the Lindbergh baby; this was repeated week after week in their papers.

Operating in conjunction with the spurious Protocols was the pseudo-scientific doctrine of race. As originally conceived in the mid-nineteenth century by a French aristocrat, Comte de Gobineau, race doctrine was an attempt to ward off rising democracy. According to Gobineau, only the aristocracy had pure Aryan blood—the source of all greatness and virtue. Mixing of blood could only mean degeneration; inequality was desirable in that it preserved the better classes. Gobineau's aim was to lend the immutability of race to class, but his successors, like the Englishman H. S. Chamberlain, simply concentrated on the idea of a superior race. Chamberlain's hymn of praise for the Teutonic or Nordic master race was appropriately set to music by his father-in-law, Richard Wagner. Strange as it may seem, Chamberlain and other pre-Hitler racists made much of the freedom-loving nature of the Teutons. Freedom of speech and of association—indeed, individual liberty itself—were enlisted under the banner of the race doctrine. But the Anglo-Saxon racists' affinity for the liberal ideals falls into place if we interpret laissez-faire liberalism as a special licence for the strong. (Seen from another angle, excessive individualism develops into the cult of personality and ultimately the fuehrer principle.) Hitler, needless to say, allowed the theme of individual liberty to languish and concentrated on the simpler idea of anti-semitism that was inherent in the doctrine of race.

Like others of their ilk before and since, Arcand and Ménard relied on the forged Protocols to do much of their propaganda work for them, and distributed copies in large numbers. They also appropriated the *achat chez nous* idea. A typical example is an open letter to housewives in *Le Miroir* (May 22, 1932), enjoining them not to buy food from Jewish storekeepers, who were libelled as "dirty," "thieves," and purveyors of germ-laden meat. At the same time the paper was running a smear campaign against Maurice Pollack, the owner of Quebec City's largest department store. Arcand's wife who organized boycotts against Jewish stores in Montreal, once obliged a reporter with a description of her methods. "It's pretty simple," she said. "You just buttonhole the customers and tell them what the Jews are doing to Canada, so they leave."[3]

Economic nationalism created a ready-made constituency for Arcand. Commercial travellers and small shopkeepers were predisposed to dislike Jews because they competed with them. It is not surprising to find that both a branch of the Catholic Association of Commercial Travellers and a group of Montreal small businessmen and doctors, led by the city's future mayor, Adhémar Raynault, had lobbied against the Bercovitch bill. Owing to economic rivalry, these groups were naturally attracted to an anti-semitic movement; in turn the movement catered to this client group. By espousing the cause of the French-Canadian businessman, Arcand could hope for much wider support as well. The rank and file of French Canadians, led by the parish priests, endorsed the *achat chez nous* campaign. Arcand's platform was calculated to attract adherents.

E. C. Hughes, a sociologist who studied the textile town of Drummondville, Quebec, in the thirties, attributed French-Canadian anti-semitism in part to the fact that the Jew served as a surrogate Englishman. While English Canadians were too powerful to attack, Jews could be attacked "without fear either of retaliation or of a bad conscience." Hughes wrote:

> Observation throughout the period leads me to conclude that the symbolic Jew receives the more bitter of the attacks which the French Canadians would like to make upon the English or perhaps even upon some of their own leaders and institutions. . . . Many of the accusations made against the Jew in Quebec—with the obvious exception of Communist leanings—

would be justified if made against the English. The department stores, chain stores, banks, and large industrial and utility corporations have been introduced and are controlled by Anglo-Saxons. The Jew in Quebec is the physically present small competitor rather than the hidden wirepuller of high finance and big business. The Jew operates and competes upon the French-Canadian businessman's own level; it is the English who have introduced the new forms of economic enterprise which threaten the French-Canadian way of living and working.[4]

Many French Canadians who continued to hold neutral or moderate views on Jews would have gone along with Arcand for the sake of his economic nationalism. People do not have to be anti-semites to support an anti-semitic program; they may regard it as subsidiary to the main issue.

But for Arcand the campaign against the Jews was *the* issue. He found his political credo in Hitler's *Mein Kampf*, particularly in the premise that Jews have no right to be citizens and therefore can be expelled from any country. Arcand's objective was the expulsion of the Jews, but in the early stages he sought to achieve his ends through political propaganda rather than political power. Goglus were urged to spread anti-Jewish material and to support a Jewish boycott. In this way he planned to create a public opinion that would deprive Canadian Jews of their rights and ultimately drive them out of the country.[5] The Patriotic Order of Goglus can most accurately be described as a proto-fascist, promotional group manipulated by a publicist. It was once remarked of Arcand that he was his own Goebbels.

In the summer of 1932, Joseph Cohen, the lawyer who had seconded the Bercovitch bill, decided to test the adequacy of the courts to deal with racial slander. In its violent criticism of the bill, the press had insisted that the law as it stood was sufficient to protect the rights of minorities. The premier and politicians from both parties had agreed. So, in the name of a Lachine merchant, Cohen brought an action against Arcand and Ménard for injuring the reputation of Jewish businessmen in the province. He sought remedy by injunction rather than damages because he said he knew from experience that the defendants would simply pay up and repeat the libel.

Arcand was hard-pressed to meet the costs of litigation. Hoping for contributions from his readers, his papers announced a "defence fund." At the same time he turned to the Conservative party. On June 4, 1932, he wrote the prime minister a desperate letter concluding with the information that "our friend Dr. Lalanne has done enormously for us and can do nothing more."[6] Influential Conservatives followed up his plea with letters of their own. Leslie Bell, M.P. for St. Antoine and a power in the party, reminded the prime minister of Arcand's "efficient and valuable service" during the last federal election, and asked Bennett to meet with Arcand and Dr. Lalanne.[7] Another English-speaking Montreal M.P., John A. Sullivan, also pressed the prime minister: "Mr. Arcand is without exception the best French-Canadian writer and his paper is making great headway. It would be a pity to see it fall."[8] Yet another advocate was the ardent nationalist, Armand Lavergne, who advised Bennett that "Arcand and his paper are together important."[9] (According to Arcand, Lavergne contributed unsigned articles to both *Le Goglu* and *Le Miroir*.)[10] Arcand also had some good friends in the Senate, notably the Speaker, Senator P. E. Blondin, who consistently urged Bennett to finance Arcand's papers more generously.[11] This support in the House and the Senate sits uncomfortably considering the nature of Arcand's publications.

The case against Arcand was heard by Mr. Justice Gonzalve Desaulniers, who was openly sympathetic to the plaintiff's cause. While giving due recognition to freedom of expression, he stated that "it is certain these three papers do a grave wrong to a section of the population; there should be some means of putting restraint on them." He also took issue with the Court of Appeal decision in the *Ortenberg* v. *Plamondon* case that a collectivity could not sue for libel. It appeared to him that when *Le Goglu* wrote that Jews are assassins, a person could say "I am a Jew, therefore they are saying that I am an assassin." However, the judge's initial courage seemed to flag under the attack of the defence lawyers. In particular, he was impressed by the argument that the plaintiffs were asking the court to decree a statute refused by the legislature, and the reminder (hardly respectful of the bench) that "judges should bend in front of the law of which they are the slaves." At this, he began to anguish over liberty of the press, and all Cohen's arguments about licence in the name of liberty were to no avail. By morning's end, the judge was reduced to stating that if he had the power he would grant the injunction, but he must examine the law. Accordingly, judgment was postponed until September. In the meantime, he asked the proprietor of the three papers not to print anything against the Jewish people. He was no more successful in obtaining voluntary compliance than Premier Taschereau had been. Taking the stand, Ménard flatly replied that he would print whatever Monsieur Arcand wished to write.[12]

Early in September Mr. Justice Desaulniers delivered his judgment. With obvious regret he rejected the request for an injunction. After due consideration he had concluded that there was no legal redress for members of a slandered group; new law would have to be written to cover the matter. Notwithstanding his acknowledged lack of jurisdiction, the judge delivered a strong moral indictment against Arcand and Ménard. Not only had they refused to cease their libels pending judgment, but they had introduced a new virulence which bespattered the bench itself. And not only had they forgotten their respect for the magistracy, but, in demanding the expulsion of the Jewish people, they had forgotten the best interests of the French Canadians, whose own rights in Canada depended upon the tolerance of the majority. Then he examined some of the libels in detail, attempting to refute them with quotations from St. Paul to Bossuet. He gave his opinion that these defamatory articles could incite the population against the Jews and he compared Arcand and Ménard to the notorious anti-Dreyfusard publisher, Edouard Drumont.[13] This humane discourse brought down upon the judge's head the ready scorn of *Le Devoir*. Its new director, Georges Pelletier, compared him to a La Bruyère character who was "long, diffuse and solemn" in saying a simple thing: in this case, that Quebec law allowed no discretion to the bench to stop anybody from writing anything. Why go back to the Medes and Persians to say so, Pelletier inquired.[14]

The courts had handed the problem back to the legislature and Taschereau accepted the responsibility. Within a few days of the Desaulniers judgment, he confided to Abel Vineberg of the *Gazette* that he was going to put a stop to several kinds of objectionable journalism, including that which caused racial strife. To stem the rising anti-semitism in the province, the premier declared that the Jewish people were "here to stay."[15] They were exemplary citizens who looked after their own and respected the law. He personally condemned the campaign against them. When the Legislative Assembly opened after the New Year, a government bill was duly distributed to the members. In form the bill was an amendment to the Quebec Civil Code but what it did in effect was to redefine defamatory libel as set out in the federal Criminal Code. Like the Bercovitch bill, it proceeded by way of injunction.

Once again the press rebelled at anti-defamation legislation. Most bitterly opposed was *Le Devoir's* Pelletier, who charged that it would permit political interference with the freedom of the press. Then as now *Le Devoir* was read by people of influence; notwithstanding *La Presse's* tenfold greater circulation, it was probably the most powerful opinion-molder in the province. More imponderable a factor was Arcand himself. On the grounds that it gave criminal jurisdiction to a civil judge, he threatened to openly defy the legislation if it was passed. Deriding Taschereau's statement that the Jewish people were here to stay, he sneered that the premier often had to swallow his words.[16]

By this time Arcand was unquestionably in touch with the Nazis in Germany. The man who recruited him was Kurt Ludecke, a Nazi agent assigned to raise money and support for his party in America. An aimless character with little to recommend him except his English tailoring and a certain glibness, Ludecke was one of those who fell under Hitler's spell in the Munich days; in Hitler, he explained, "I found the answer to my lostness, my deep unrest." In the autumn of 1932 Ludecke was in Canada to find "representatives to serve as contacts" for the Nazi party: one of these was Adrien Arcand, of whom he had apparently heard from an American major who was a Nazi sympathizer. In his book, *I Knew Hitler*, Ludecke recounts how he and his American wife Mildred "drove to Montreal to keep our appointment with Adrien Arcand, the fiery leader of the 'Ordre Patriotique des Goglus'." He found the Order "a violently anti-Jewish in the main, Catholic Folkic movement, which at that time was growing rapidly in French Canada, with three publications, all very demagogic and clever." Arcand knew Ludecke by reputation, in fact had published an article of his several months earlier. They got along well together. "I liked young Arcand at once," Ludecke writes, "his vibrant, intelligent, fine-featured face, his genuine fighting spirit."[17] He presented Arcand with an autographed picture of Hitler (to be treasured and displayed at Arcand headquarters even in 1940) and Arcand reciprocated by helping Ludecke's wife to purchase a fur coat.[18] It is evident that Arcand agreed to work with the Nazis, probably in the dissemination of propaganda. "We understood each other perfectly," Ludecke records, "and agreed to co-operate in every way."

When Ludecke arrived at his Washington headquarters he passed on his high opinion of Arcand to the American major:

> You are quite right about the Goglus. They are very effective indeed in their propaganda, their cartoons as well as their literature. I had a very interesting interview with their brilliant and fiery leader, Adrien Arcand, in Montreal, and we may expect much from him, the more so as he apparently is in complete accord with Mr. Bennett, the great Prime Minister of Canada, who more and more comes to the front in British Empire politics.[19]

Evidently Arcand had promised Ludecke that he would get him an appointment with the Prime Minister of Canada. On January 4, 1933, Arcand wrote to Bennett's private secretary that "Kurt G. W. Ludecke, Hitler's representative in Washington, would be anxious to see Mr. Bennett about the third or fourth week of January. Please let me know if it is possible." Had this appointment taken place Ludecke undoubtedly would have mentioned it in his book.

Arcand's early linkage with the Nazi movement is indicated in a letter dated February 21, 1933, from a correspondent in Upper Bavaria. The occasion was Hitler's elevation to the chancellorship, and the writer felicitated with Arcand on the victory.

> I would first of all congratulate you and your fighters of the Ordre Patriotique des Goglus for having bravely carried on Hitler's mission in far away Canada, and it is a great thing to know that far out in Canada, brethren of ours are jubilant these very days of the beginning of the Renaissance of the holy north.[20]

The writer assured Arcand that Hitler would become a dictator; as a "full-blooded Nordic" he could do no less. The race doctrine was the cement that bound Nazis everywhere.

In March 1933 when Hitler did in fact become a dictator, no one inside or outside Germany was more jubilant than Adrien Arcand. He told his readers that the arrival of Hitler created "wild enthusiasm in all countries that suffer from the Jews," and he predicted that the anti-Jewish government in Germany would bring about similar governments in fifteen other countries. Readers were exhorted to stand up and be counted also:

> What about us, Goglus, do we know what to do as well as the young patriots in the European countries? Are we going to roll back the Jewish invasion more each day? Are we going to spread the word as much as we can about boycotting Jewish merchants and products? Are we going to convince our merchants not to receive Jewish travelling salesmen and not to buy anything from Jewish suppliers?[21]

So far as the editor of *Le Goglu* was concerned, the cause for celebration over Hitler's ascent to power was the official anti-semitism he immediately introduced. German Jews were to be dismissed from the civil service and disbarred; a country-wide boycott of Jewish firms was instituted. Jews were humiliated on the streets and beaten up while police stood by indulgently. In March 1933, when other Canadian newspapers were filled with stories of the perils facing German Jews, Arcand told readers of *Le Goglu* that if it was good for Germany to get rid of its Jews, it would be even better for Quebec and Canada.

While Arcand was rejoicing that all his prophesies about the Jewish fate were coming true in 1933, *Le Goglu* and the other Ménard publications were in serious financial trouble. The publisher had been involved in no less than twenty law-suits —non-Jews and Jews alike having sued him for damages—and his printing shop had had three fires, the last one having gutted it completely.[22] There is no evidence of any reputable support at this juncture for his papers. Advertising revenue had disappeared and the journals gave the appearance of an outlaw press. Ménard's affairs were in ruins. He would soon go bankrupt and, in fact was to serve a short jail sentence for libelling a non-Jewish sportscaster.[23]

But the fatal blow came from Bennett. One early morning

Senator Blondin was summoned to the prime minister's office, following which (in Blondin's own words) "I advised Arcand and Ménard that their enterprise and their papers had better be brought to an end,—and that they should turn a new sheet. Consequently their three papers, their printing establishment and their debts were liquidated."[24] In March 1933, *Le Goglu, Le Miroir* and *Le Chameau* were all closed down by Bennett's unofficial decree.

With its last gasp *Le Goglu* heaped scorn upon Taschereau's proposed bill to curb group libel. Seeking the common denominator of prejudice, Arcand discarded the idea of a Jewish world conspiracy which he had acquired from his international associates, and reverted to old themes of religious anti-semitism. Actually his fight against the group libel bill was won. The suspension of publication of the slander sheets gave Premier Taschereau the chance to extricate himself from his commitment to the Jewish community. On April 11, he announced that ·the bill would be retired because the offending papers had gone out of business. "The deplorable state of affairs no longer exists," he declared, adding that "there are some journals which do not share all our convictions but they are decent [*convenable*]."[25]

Final issues of *Le Miroir* and *Le Goglu* were devoted to an apologia for fascism as Arcand understood it. He acknowledged its ultraconservative nature; yet, instead of showing it in its true colours as the radical Right, he clothed it in the French-Canadian virtues of traditionalism and Christian piety, tracing a direct line from Catholicism through conservatism to fascism. He condemned liberalism for substituting racial and religious tolerance for what he regarded as the exclusive rights of a Christian and French-Canadian people. In singing the praises of fascism, Arcand paid R. B. Bennett the dubious compliment of comparing him to Mussolini and Hitler and finding his ideas in perfect harmony with theirs.[26]

In spite of Arcand's close links with at least a segment of the Conservative party, no prominent Conservatives were publicly identified with his openly pro-Nazi orientation in early 1933. Nor is there evidence of much popular support for him at that time. Although folk anti-semitism in French Canada provided receptivity for the early antics of *Le Goglu*, when Arcand evolved into a partisan of Hitler's he frightened away many supporters. Unlike its admiration for Mussolini, French Canada's attitude was ambivalent towards Hitler at the time he came to power. Despite Arcand's picture of him as a Christian crusader, French Canadians were suspicious of Hitler's latent anti-Catholicism. Arcand's hero worship undoubtedly made him suspect even with many who shared his anti-Jewish sentiments. Much of this distrust of the Nazi leader, however, was allayed when Pope Pius XI signed a concordat with the New Germany in the summer of 1933.

III A Fascist Movement in Quebec

As the Nazi regime went from strength to strength in its first year, there were increasing signs of anti-democratic and anti-semitic sentiment in Quebec. For one thing, the circle of ultranationalists who sat at the feet of Abbé Lionel Groulx began publishing a review called *L'Action Nationale*, in which dictatorship was praised and anti-semitic articles and commentary appeared. Actually the review was a revival of an earlier publication modelled on Charles Maurras's *L'Action Française* and bearing the same title. The Frenchman Maurras, who may be regarded as a fascist *avant la lettre*, had been a shaping influence on Groulx since the latter's graduate studies in Europe at the beginning of the century.[1] Following Maurras and others, Groulx developed a nationalism that, by its very nature, was anti-democratic and racist. He attracted a number of French-Canadian intellectuals and from 1917 to 1928 *L'Action Française* was the vehicle of their ideas. In 1933 the review was reborn as *L'Action Nationale*. Although it had a circulation of less than two thousand, this was no measure of its influence. Its real strength lay in the support it received from influential papers like *Le Devoir, L'Action Catholique* and *Le Droit*.

Under the *nom de plume* of "Jacques Brassier" Abbé Groulx wrote a regular column for the new review, many of which dealt with the need for a strong man. "Happy peoples who have found dictators," he wrote in the January 1934 issue. And in November of the same year, he quoted one of his own speeches wherein he lauded Mussolini, and added that "if at present Il Duce's regime offers some stability, it is owing to the young generation of Italians who were formed according to the methods of fascism." While Groulx may have longed for a French-Canadian dictator, he did not overtly preach anti-semitism. He espoused the *achat chez nous* campaign vigorously, however, and his strongly nationalist views, taken to their logical conclusion by his followers, inspired a racist xenophobia.

The new review's anti-semitism went far beyond the *achat chez nous* movement. Writing in the September 1933 issue, one of its directors, Anatole Vanier, advocated depriving Jewish citizens of their full civil and political rights and treating them as a group apart. Not only did he want to cut off Jewish immigration at a time when refugees were starting to flow out of Nazi Germany, but he wanted to deny naturalization to Jews and to take away from the Canadian-born their franchise and rights of citizenship. According to the editor of *L'Action Nationale*, the Vanier article was "much appreciated" and received favourable comment in local papers.[2]

In seeking to turn Jewish Canadians into second-class citizens, the *L'Action Nationale* coterie was in step with Arcand. An analysis of the review's position on Jews in 1933–34 reveals the Jewish issues as they appeared to the racist-nationalist groups. One allegation was that the politicians had made the Jews a privileged caste, allotting two seats in the provincial legislature to the Jewish district in Montreal instead of amalgamating them into one. As a corollary to this, it was alleged that Jews tampered with election returns. A second charge was that the Jewish merchants monopolized commerce and were aided by the law that allowed them to keep open Sunday in lieu of their Saturday sabbath. Third, that Jews had taken over the professions, and that a more rigorous quota system in the universities was necessary. Fourth, that Jews had no right to seek representation on the Protestant school board. This raised the question of Jewish minority rights which the nationalists wished to withhold. Fifth, that Jews were pro-communist. Although communism was an insignificant movement in Quebec province, the Catholic church's anathema had created an attitude to it of almost pathological fear. Finally, with the persecution of the Jews in Germany, the question of Jewish immigration became a live issue. Historically, French Canada was opposed to immigration, and in the depths of the Depression, Canada as a whole had become xenophobic; but the reaction of *L'Action Nationale* was hostile in the extreme. On June 5, 1933, the *Ligue d'Action Nationale*—the organizational structure of the review's supporters—forwarded a resolution to the federal government protesting any Jewish immigration in these terms:

> That the Canadian borders be kept completely closed indefinitely in these days of general unemployment which weighs so heavily on the national budget; that the government of Canada remain perfectly inflexible before Jewish pressure of any kind, national or worldwide, so that no complaisance be shown in favour of an element accused of Marxism and Communism by Germany, and which in itself cannot be an asset for Canada, being by its faith, its customs and its character unassimilable, a source of division and dispute, and thus of weakness for the Canadian people.[3]

Meanwhile racist nationalism had flared up in the classical colleges and the University of Montreal. A handful of the more militant students formed a political action group calling itself *Les Jeune-Canada*; it was a kind of junior auxilliary to the Groulx circle. Like their elders, these young intellectuals were disgusted with the political system which they felt favoured the English and the Jews over native French Canadians. They admired Mussolini and yearned for a leader. In the winter of 1933 the group began to hold public meetings and to deliver radio broadcasts. All their activities received generous coverage in *Le Devoir*, in particular their vociferous opposition to a Jewish rally at the Montreal Arena.

On April 6 the Jewish community of Montreal sponsored a rally at the Arena to protest Hitler's treatment of the German Jews. Presided over by the mayor, it was attended by a provincial cabinet minister and a senator. Present also were the Anglican bishop and a Presbyterian minister, but the Catholic clergy was conspicuously absent. Mayor Rinfret set the theme in his opening remarks about liberty and the rights of minorities. Commending the cultural contribution of the German Jews, he stated that Germany had stained its flag with its persecution of this minority. He was followed by the three Jewish members of Parliament. S. W. Jacobs explained that it was not the isolated acts of violence that were so disturbing; it was the loss of citizenship rights placing the German Jews outside the law in their own country. A. A. Heaps blamed the German government, not the people, while Sam Factor proposed various practical steps such as a Canadian protest through the League of Nations or non-renewal of the Canadian-German trade treaty. Honoré Mercier, representing the Taschereau government, stressed Quebec's traditional tolerance. His assurance that there was "no place here for prejudices of race, language or religion" may have sounded suspiciously like wishful thinking to many of his audience. The extremely popular Senator Dandurand received a standing ovation. Speaking of his days as president of the League of Nations Assembly, he told how the German delegates had always championed the cause of minority rights at Geneva. He professed himself unable to understand their "present demagoguery," and chose to regard it as "a passing epidemic of hysteria." That Germany might take a different attitude towards German minorities abroad and the Jewish minority at home apparently did not occur to the venerable statesman. Another speaker warmly received by the gathering was the Anglican bishop; in fact it was Bishop Farthing who proposed a resolution asking the Prime Minister of Canada to "take such measures as he judges opportune in the circumstances" and to communicate with Great Britain on possible joint action.[4]

It was this display of liberalism that provoked the violent reaction of *Les Jeune-Canada*. In a public statement, carried in full in *Le Devoir*, the young nationalists protested the fact that politicians had attended the Jewish rally.

> The Jews can agitate as much as they wish, that is their business, but our people had no right to engage the reputation and the interests of all our nation to defend a group of immigrants.[5]

On April 21, *Les Jeune-Canada* held a counter-protest meeting at the *Salle du Gesu*. One after another, the leaders spoke on the "Jewish question" in Canada, among them, a youthful André Laurendeau, who was to change his opinion after seeing fascism and Nazism at first hand during his studies in Europe. Although a number of newspapers refused to carry any publicity about the meeting, *Les Jeune-Canada's* public anti-semitism was encouraged by *Le Devoir* and *L'Action Nationale*. According to the latter, the young men spoke for a policy of national interest and prudent democracy over "a short-sighted and absurd" liberalism.

While *Les Jeune-Canada* could hardly be accused of Nazism, another group seemed to invite such a label. In 1933 a workers' organization, the *Fédération des Clubs Ouvriers*, suddenly donned brown shirts and openly espoused fascism. On the strength of a program that was anti-trust, nationalistic, and strongly anti-semitic, the *Fédération* immediately ventured into municipal politics, running a candidate in a Montreal by-election. These self-announced fascists came to public attention with a huge Easter Sunday parade to St. Joseph's Oratory. The leader was a financially distressed white-collar worker named Chalifoux.[6] Although the group's main strength was in Montreal, they attracted some followers in the nearby towns. T. D. Bouchard, then mayor of St. Hyacinthe, recalls in his *Mémoires* how Brownshirts marched about plastering store windows with anti-Jewish signs, although he adds that they were a negligible factor in the town of 40,000.[7] Consistent with its aims, the *Fédération* was vocal in opposing the entry of Jewish refugees into Canada. In August 1933 the *Montreal Gazette* reported that the St. Edouard section of the Federation of Labour Clubs had passed a strong anti-immigration resolution. The article went on to say that brown shirts and fascist salutes were much in evidence at the meeting.

Surprisingly, Arcand did not embrace the *Fédération des Clubs Ouvriers*. He fought it from the beginning, maintaining that it was the tool of big business and of a certain clique in the Conservative party. The underlying purpose of its backers, he claimed, was to head off a genuine fascist movement in the province; using Chalifoux as a front, they had created an imitation fascism. "Those who play this game," wrote Arcand, "hope in this way to paralyse THE OTHER which has a definite program and knows where it is going."[8]

Arcand meant no other than himself. Inspired by Hitler, he had mapped out plans for a Nazi-style movement in Quebec. In fact, he and Ménard were once again publishing their hate propaganda. Somewhere they had found backing for a new weekly, *Le Patriote*, which proclaimed that it was "carrying on the anti-democratic campaign of *Le Miroir*."[9] The first issue on May 4, 1933, named the enemies: liberalism, communism, socialism, bolshevism—and behind all these, the Jew. Readers were notified that "the principal end of *Le Patriote* will be to disengage our race from anti-Christian poison and help us to return to the sources of our strength in our past."

Early issues of *Le Patriote* set the scene for the emergence of Arcand's Nazi-style party. There were editorial sighs for a strong leader, coupled with extravagant admiration for Mussolini and Hitler—"the liberator." There was a running battle with Chalifoux's *Fédération des Clubs Ouvriers*, which had to be weakened or destroyed before "the other" fascism could emerge. In the autumn Arcand and Ménard began sponsoring public meetings once more, on such topics as "Fascism or Socialism." They also spoke throughout the province on "the Jewish Question," often under the auspices of the St. Jean-Baptiste Society. A special effort was made to enlist University of Montreal students (many of whom belonged to *Les Jeune-Canada*). In the early autumn, *Le Patriote* announced that it was going to hold a meeting for them, and all who attended would be furnished with swastika buttons. This link with the students suggests that Arcand may have had something to do with the violent racial nationalism of *Les Jeune-Canada*. It is a fact that *Le Goglu* had had many youthful admirers.

In the face of this anti-semitic activity, the Canadian Jewish Congress, dormant for some time, was reorganized under the presidency of the Montreal M.P., S. W. Jacobs. On Boxing Day, 1933, Jacobs wrote to a friend in Baltimore sadly reflecting that "in the period covering my whole life I have never seen anything so virulent as the campaign which is being propagated against Jews in the Province of Quebec." He firmly believed that money was coming from Berlin. Addressing the newly formed Congress he said:

> Quebec papers waging an anti-semitic campaign are subsidized from Germany. Not one person carrying on an anti-Jewish campaign in Quebec is a man of responsibility. Many are mere youths, not yet twenty. Quebec public men are with us. But we must watch that this anti-semitism does not spread as it did in Germany. Pictures of Hitler are flaunted in the editorial offices of Quebec papers attacking Jews. We have one paper in Quebec worse in its attitude to Jews than any in Germany. It must be subsidized, for prior to its present campaign against Jewry it was dragged through the bankruptcy courts. No decent firm would advertise in such columns.[10]

It is unlikely that Jacobs had proof of this charge; but he deduced that it was true from Ménard's recent bankruptcy, *Le Patriote's* visible lack of advertising income and its strong pro-Hitler editorial policy.

Certainly Arcand had close ties with Germany since Ludecke's visit of the previous year; also he was in touch with a number of German propaganda agencies which sent him material. Moreover, in a letter to an American fascist dated September 28, 1933, he stated that *Le Patriote* was known to Hitler and was very well appreciated by the Nazi propaganda bureau.[11] But there is no evidence that he was subsidized by the Nazis, at least at this stage.

It was early in 1934 that, following many broad hints, *Le Patriote* finally announced the formation of *Le Parti National Social Chrétien* (the National Social Christian Party) under the leadership of its editor, Adrien Arcand. A mixture of German and Italian fascism, the new party promised law and order, corporatism and social justice, with a Grand Council to take over the administration of the country from a "bankrupt" democracy. Editorializing on the need for the new party, Arcand identified the following he hoped to win as the small businessman, the worker and the farmer.

The first meeting took place on February 22 at the Monument National in Montreal. From its inception, the movement patterned its style on Nazism. The hall was decorated with swastika flags forming the party's initials, and a double line of blue-uniformed followers, known as the *Casques d'Acier* or Steel Helmets after the German war veterans' organization, held aloft swastika banners through which Arcand marched to the stage. Introduced by Ménard, the self-proclaimed leader was the sole speaker of the evening. Arcand's theme was that democracy could not cope with the Depression—a proposition that bore a semblance of truth at a time when 20 per cent of the country's workers were unemployed. From there he launched into the real business of the meeting, which was to stir up anti-semitism. The new party would regulate "the Jewish Question" when it came to power. Jews would no longer be citizens; in fact they would be shipped off to Palestine or to a colony at Hudson's Bay (by train and "comfortable" dog sled).[12] Arcand later admitted that this first audience was not caught up in his own fervour. Nevertheless, they had come to see a show and he proved that he could give them one.

In spite of the fact that Arcand's Patriotic Order of Goglus had evolved into a Nazi-style shirt movement, some high-ranking Quebec Conservatives were still trying to foist him on Bennett. Shortly after Arcand's meeting at the Monument National, Senator Blondin wrote to the prime minister: "By means of public lectures and intensive publicity, he [Arcand] has launched a movement which under the name of 'The Christian National Party' aims simply at the debunking of all the rot in the old parties,—which, when the end comes, will be found to be 'a regenerated Conservative party' in Quebec,—which I think we need." Was Blondin suggesting that the Conservatives harness the new movement for its own uses? After praising *Le Patriote* as being on a much higher level than Arcand's former publications and also "more powerful," the Speaker of the Senate concluded with a glowing tribute to Arcand the man: "With no paper in Quebec worth mentioning and with no man of the size, and power, and moral character of Arcand, do not you think that, at least, he should not be completely ignored?"[13] Another who wrote to the prime minister on Arcand's behalf at this time was J. E. Laforce, the president of the St. Jean-Baptiste Society. He suggested that there was a possibility of obtaining the services of Mr. Arcand as editor of a Conservative paper.[14]

For the next few months the new party and its official organ were devoted to the task of getting Arcand's lawyer, Salluste Lavery, elected mayor of Montreal. Lavery, whose connection with Arcand dates back to the first issues of *Le Goglu*, in which he was an advertiser, was running on an openly anti-Jewish platform. It is instructive to see the groups which (according to *Le Patriote*) were supporting him. In addition to Arcand's National Social Christian Party, there were *La Ligue du Dimanche* (whose purpose was to press for Sunday store closings), the St. Jean-Baptiste Society, the Commercial Travellers' Association, the largest Catholic youth organization (the ACJC), *Les Jeune-Canada*, the Catholic labour unions, and the *Fédération des Clubs Ouvriers*.[15] In addition, he probably had the votes of many members of the Native Sons of Canada, an organization in which he was active all his life. Lavery was soundly defeated by Camillien Houde; but Arcand called it a great victory for the fascists because their candidate polled a tenth of the vote.

Although an anti-semitic platform did not win a mayoralty election in 1934, anti-semitism was very active in Montreal. A case in point was the forced resignation of a Jewish intern from a Catholic hospital. When his appointment to the staff became known in June, it touched off a walk-out of the other interns. At first determined to stick it out, the young intern's resolve began to falter when the doctors at five other Catholic hospitals joined in the strike. When the combined nursing staff of all these hospitals threatened to walk off the job also, he was forced to resign.[16] The incident illustrates dramatically the economic rivalry that underlay so much of the anti-semitism in Quebec as elsewhere, and which fed the springs of the fascist movement.

Meanwhile the Canadian Jewish Congress had not been idle. Mainly through the untiring efforts of its executive secretary, H. M. Caiserman, a campaign to stop the fascists had been mounted on various fronts. Lavery's anti-semitic electioneering on the radio had been checked by a letter to the chairman of the Canadian Radio Broadcasting Commission, Hector Charlesworth.[17] Similarly, on learning that Arcand and Lavery were holding mass meetings in a number of churches, Caiserman contacted the elected representatives for those districts and some of the meetings, at least, were cancelled.[18] Plans were afoot to commission the poet A. M. Klein to prepare a refutation of the Protocols for translation into French, to organize a boycott of German goods in cooperation with the American Jewish Congress, and to make another effort to obtain anti-defamation legislation either at the federal or provincial level.[19]

Jacobs had a host of French-Canadian acquaintances and he turned to them in what he clearly regarded as a serious situation. He sought the advice, among others, of the senior statesman, Henri Bourassa. Early in the century, Bourassa had had a not unearned reputation for anti-semitism; however he claimed that reading the anti-Dreyfusard Edouard Drumont had cured him. Indeed, he had made the statement that *Le Devoir* would never campaign against the Jews as long as he managed it.[20] Although the paper's handling of the Bercovitch bill seemed to negate this promise, shortly afterwards Bourassa had stepped down as director and had immediately given a public lecture in favour of social justice for the Jews. (In fact, Bourassa's concern over human rights moved Arcand to call him "a Jew-lover like his grandfather Papineau."[21]) In April 1934 a meeting took place in Jacobs' office between Congress officials and the respected French-Canadian leader; the upshot, to Caiserman's delight, was that Bourassa made "a marvellous address in condemnation of anti-semitism" in the House of Commons.[22] Yet notwithstanding all the efforts at changing attitudes, it is probable that the Jewish Congress's most effective move in combatting Arcand and Ménard was "an educational campaign" among *Le Patriote's* advertisers, pointing out the dangers of the fascist ideology. Caiserman reported "a noble response."

This may partially explain why, less than a year after its inception, *Le Patriote* was floundering in financial difficulties. In July 1934 Ménard appealed for help to his readers. He confessed that the paper had only one paid advertisement, the rest were complimentary. If $1,000 in gifts or subscriptions was not forthcoming, *Le Patriote* would disappear like its predecessors. The response could at most be called a trickle. A month later only $86 had been raised. Nevertheless the paper kept going. Somewhere there was a mysterious patron.

Funds were also found for a second party rally in October. Arcand had now organized a corps of Blueshirts who, it was announced, would keep order at the meeting.[23] Like Sir Oswald Mosley's rallies in England, Arcand's were to be characterized by violence, provoked by his uniformed supporters. While he and his "indefatigable collaborator" were better pleased by the response to this meeting, it received little press coverage and the Canadian Nazi movement was still not off the ground. Even an announcement that they had established links with fascists in Western Canada failed to make news.[24]

Nevertheless, the National Social Christian Party was on the move. *Le Patriote* now had a regular correspondent in the Ottawa-Hull area and the party had a local leader in the person of an Ottawa policeman, Jean Tissot.[25] Tissot devoted his off-duty hours to distributing fascist propaganda and to promoting a boycott of Jewish stores. For these extra-curricular activities he was suspended from the police force.[26] Possibly he wrote the Ottawa column in *Le Patriote* himself. Its one and only theme was an attack on local Jewish merchants, in particular on A. J. Freiman, owner of Ottawa's largest department store and president of the Zionist Council of Canada.

Arcand's propaganda against the Jewish people aroused more opposition in Ottawa than in Montreal. Both English-language daily newspapers deplored the circulation of anti-semitic pamphlets in the capital. The *Ottawa Journal* hoped that "possibly they do little harm, because racial prejudice is foreign to the Canadian tradition and abhorrent to all instincts of fairness and decency." But, the editorial warned, "such attacks do represent a deplorable attempt to duplicate in this country bitterness and enmities that have their origin in other lands and they should be suppressed sternly."[27] The *Ottawa Citizen* saw national security implications in *Le Patriote's* continuing anti-semitic rant:

> It is astonishing to find Canadian people lending themselves to . . . racial animosity in this country. Canadian economic conditions are sufficiently deplorable without being made worse by internal strife based on nothing more substantial than the colour of a man's hair or the accident of birth into one religious faith or another. Seeds are sown, however, for civil disorder on this basis of race prejudice. There is evidence of it even in Ottawa, where an appeal is being circulated particularly to French-speaking people by a vile propaganda sheet from Montreal. It is so obviously designed to distract Canada with difficulties at home, when the Nazi bid is made for world power, it is difficult to believe that Canadian people would allow themselves to be misled by it.[28]

There can be little doubt that Arcand had become emboldened by the renewed attentions of some very prominent politicians. The country was heading into an election, and the beleaguered Bennett administration was hastily trying to put together an organization. Once again Senator Rainville called upon Arcand's services. He appointed him publicity director for Bennett's campaign in Quebec.

Meanwhile several of Arcand's fascist friends were running under the banner of H. H. Stevens, the former Conservative cabinet minister who had broken away from Bennett to found the Reconstruction party. As chairman of the Royal Commission on Price Spreads, Stevens had become the champion of the small businessman against the chains and department stores. Whether he wished it or not, this earned him *Le Patriote's* salute as a man of "fascist temperament and spirit." Stevens was no fascist, but expediency forced him to travel into the election with several of Arcand's followers. For instance, in Montreal Salluste Lavery was a Reconstruction party candidate running against S. W. Jacobs, and in Ottawa, the fascist ex-policeman, Jean Tissot, was contesting a seat as an Independent favouring the Reconstruction party.

To the expressed surprise of many of Le Patriote's readers, the paper officially supported Stevens while its editor openly campaigned for Bennett.[29] In his party's bulletin, Le Fasciste Canadien, Arcand told his followers that a second term for Bennett would provide the transition to their own party, and that Bennett's New Deal would usher in corporatism. While most Conservatives were "shocked and startled" (in the words of the Montreal Gazette) by Bennett's radical program which he broadcasted on the eve of the election, Arcand rejoiced in the belief that "all the Bennett legislation tends towards fascism."[30] Certainly, government control and regulation were as much the essence of fascism as of socialism, and Arcand approved of the proposed boards and commissions. Like the European dictators, however, Arcand's view of state control included co-existence with capitalism. For him, the destruction of property rights was the ultimate sin of socialism. Thus he could not tolerate Aberhart, the newly elected premier of Alberta, because he believed that the Social Credit scheme to hand out $25 a month to every Albertan would lead to a gradual confiscation of private wealth. When some of Aberhart's party men approached Arcand for propaganda to use against the banks and financiers, he spurned them.[31] He later modified this position when he saw that Social Credit was far from a socialist movement.*

In Bennett's service, Arcand fought a virulent publicity campaign against Mackenzie King, linking him with Stalin and anti-Christ in the immoderate fashion he usually reserved for Jews. His campaign consisted of reviling King for his pledge to repeal the notorious section 98 of the Criminal Code,[32] which allowed the police to break up meetings of alleged communists and to arrest them on the barest suspicion. It was legislation that had been framed in the anti-communist hysteria of the Winnipeg General Strike. Of the three party leaders, only Bennett was in favour of keeping section 98.

---

*After the Second World War, Arcand made political overtures to various Social Credit members of parliament. (P.A.C., Collection Arcand, vol. 3).

While Arcand issued pamphlet after pamphlet for the Bennett campaign, *Le Patriote* churned out articles in support of Stevens. Curiously, the ailing fascist organ revived during election year, even expanding its operations with an English edition for the Ottawa area. Both French and English editions were largely devoted to promoting the campaign of the Reconstruction party candidates. Montreal readers were told that "all Christians should cast their vote for Salluste Lavery . . . and the Jew Jacobs will disappear from the political scene as if by magic." The Ottawa edition offered such headlines as "Christian or Jew? Tissot or Freiman?"

Indeed, Tissot was in the midst of his campaign when Freiman launched a slander suit against him. *Le Patriote's* attacks on this highly respected merchant had become progressively worse and Tissot peddled the publication widely throughout the city. Because he was specifically named in these defamatory articles, Freiman was able to invoke the libel section of the Criminal Code. On October 9, 1935, the Ontario Supreme Court found Tissot guilty of criminal libel. At the jury trial it came out that he had attempted to incite non-Jewish merchants against Freiman. The managing director of a large store testified that the defendant had tried to solicit funds from him to form an association of Christian merchants whose objective it would be to drive all Jewish storekeepers out of Ottawa. Tissot, however, had misjudged the spirit of competition among Ottawa businessmen, for the witness told the court he had promptly informed Mr. Freiman of the slander being circulated against him.[33]

Not surprisingly Tissot lost his election as well as his lawsuit. In fact, all Arcand's friends and associates fared badly at the polls. The Bennett government was turned out and Stevens alone of the Reconstruction party was elected. Arcand wasted no tears over his fallen heroes. *Le Fasciste Canadien* informed party members that the National Social Christian Party was the heir of the Conservatives, that although the old party was broken, the instincts of the Right survived and these would devolve upon the fascist party. However, he did not promise immediate victory. Canada would only go fascist he said, when the suffering and terror imposed by the communists was clearly apparent. As in Italy and Germany, Canadians would have to realize the dangers of the extreme Left before seeking the protection of the extreme Right.

V Swastika Clubs in Ontario

Hitler's rise to power in the spring of 1933 not only inspired Arcand to transform his Patriotic Order of Goglus into a genuine fascist movement, it also caused fascist stirrings in other parts of Canada. In Ontario, Swastika Clubs suddenly sprang up—gangs of youths wearing swastika badges who harassed Jewish people on public beaches and in the parks. In Manitoba, the manifestations of Nazism were of a more adult and disturbing kind. As in Quebec, a shirt group—the Canadian Nationalist Party—was operating openly. From 1933 to 1935 the western fascists were actually more numerous and better organized than Arcand's party. English Canada was shocked at every reminder of Swastika Clubs and fascist parties in its midst, and persisted in regarding them as totally alien to its democratic way of life (while quite at home in Quebec). But fascism west of the Ottawa River was not just an import. English-speaking Canadians themselves indulged to some degree in its main component—racism.

Apart from the French enclave in Quebec, Canada in the 1930s was visibly a British country. By law Canadians were British subjects; indeed, Canadian nationality remained a fuzzy matter legally until the Canadian Citizenship Act of 1947. To describe Canada between the wars as a pluralistic society was inapt. Although the phrase "Canadian mosaic" had recently been coined, pressure to assimilate to the Anglo-Saxon model was overwhelming. Those of non-British origin were regarded as Canadians only in so far as they approximated to the model. A reverence for British institutions and an acceptance of British standards characterized the period. But the British tradition of freedom and self-government was thought to be properly understood only by those of Anglo-Saxon heritage. The arbiter of all actions was "British fair play" and this was constantly invoked by all Canadians regardless of national origin. Travelling across the country in the thirties, an observer of ethnic communities found that "English influence permeates all Canadian life."[1] Ethnic names were few in the legislatures and unknown in board rooms. Newspaper social columns chronicled the life of an exclusively Anglo-Saxon society.

Those of British origin actually represented barely more than half the population. Mass immigration both before and after the 1914 war had brought hundreds of thousands of newcomers from eastern and central Europe. Around 1930 this demographic change became a major issue in the country. People were afraid that European immigration would change the texture of the Canadian population and endanger British primacy.[2] Indeed, fears that Canada was changing to a multicultural country led to the less than subtle assertion of British superiority known as Anglo-Saxon nativism. "Keep Canada British" was the popular slogan of the times. This nationalistic sentiment was reinforced by the familiar theories of biological superiority. There was a great deal written and spoken about the "Anglo-Saxon race," accompanied by an upsurge of interest in the pseudo-science of eugenics.

The Depression aggravated these tendencies into a national xenophobia. High unemployment ended the open door policy, and henceforth only Anglo-Saxons were welcome. With the advent of the Bennett government in the summer of 1930, British preference became official. Speaking to the Canadian Club in Toronto, the Minister of Immigration, W. A. Gordon, told a sympathetic audience:

> I am afraid the past has revealed in a large measure an undisciplined encouragement of the entry into Canada of people, many of whom I am afraid are incapable of being assimilated into and of understanding the social, the religious and political structure that has been built up in our country.[3]

Two weeks later the same audience heard an imperialist address that was the corollary to the Gordon speech. Looking ahead to the time when immigration would be resumed, Commissioner Turner of the Salvation Army declared:

> I am sure you . . . will want to give preference to British people, blood of your own blood and kin of your own kin, and by getting the right kind of people into this country and having them properly absorbed and taken care of you will bring up the right kind of nation that will do yourselves credit and do the country credit and as a united Empire we will march on to victory.

Toronto was the stronghold of Anglo-Saxon nativism. The most British city in Canada, 81 per cent of its 631,207 people were of British stock; of these, 55 per cent came from England. It was the headquarters of the Orange Order, whose militant Protestantism and imperialistic fervour as yet showed little signs of abatement. Orange Day parades were mammoth affairs, with eight to ten thousand marchers and a hundred thousand spectators. Although the Orangemen aimed their biggest guns at their traditional enemy, the French Canadians, they also took a strong stand against European immigrants who—to quote a twelfth of July orator—"have no knowledge of our love of civil and religious liberty."[4]

The xenophobia of Toronto's British Canadians was primarily directed at the Jewish community of 45,000. The cause was the upward mobility of this ethnic group. There were some Jewish people who had prospered in the 1920s and, by the early thirties, were seeking to acquire the amenities of the comfortable classes, such as nice homes in good residential districts and vacations at the better resorts. This caused resentment among the dominant Anglo-Saxon group which had previously monopolized these good things. In the 1950s sociologist Dennis Wrong wrote that:

> Twenty years ago one often heard respectable middle-class non-Jews make blatantly anti-semitic remarks that were repeated by their children at the better private schools and the elite university fraternities and sororities. The social atmosphere of upper middle-class Toronto, while genteel in tone, was thoroughly anti-semitic, although probably no more so than in several other North American cities at the time.[5]

The economic status of Toronto Jews, who formed 5.7 per cent of the city's population in 1931, hardly justified the feeling against them. Residentially, they remained ghetto-bound in two downtown wards; of the better districts, only the new suburb of Forest Hill had more than a sprinkling. Most Jews either owned or worked in small stores or workshops; there were virtually none in management positions in the chain stores or department stores or in the larger industrial enterprises. And, despite the common assumption that they had taken over the professions, only 3 per cent of Toronto's professional people were Jewish. As teaching and nursing were virtually closed to them, they were concentrated in professions where they could be self-employed. This created a rising trend towards careers in law and medicine, and in 1931 5 per cent of Toronto doctors and 9.5 per cent of its lawyers were Jewish. Although 5 per cent of those engaged in insurance and real estate were Jewish, an abnormally low proportion became managers or officials, and the same bar to advancement held true for Jewish brokers in stocks and bonds. The proportion of Jews employed by banks and loan companies actually dropped from 1921 to 1931.[6]

In 1933 the *Toronto Star* followed up a charge that the banks were boycotting Jewish help. Bank officials denied it, giving various reasons for the conspicuous absence of this group on staff: Jews did not want to go to small towns; Jews felt they could earn more money in commerce; Jews were gregarious and liked to be with their own race.[7] The statistician for the Canadian Jewish Congress, Louis Rosenberg, brushed aside such explanations based on assumed racial traits. "It has been claimed," he wrote,

> that Jews do not willingly accept subordinate positions in banks, but this excuse would be disproved very speedily by the large number of qualified young Jewish men who would fall over themselves to apply for such positions in banks even at prevailing salaries, if it were rumoured that there were a possibility of Jews being accepted.

As for the myth, beloved of fascists, that Jews controlled the financial world in Canada, statistics show them to have been a totally negligible factor. Less than one per cent of the directors of Canadian corporations were Jewish, and these were mostly on the boards of small companies or privately incorporated family concerns. No Jew sat on the board of the prestigious transportation or utility companies. Stock exchanges were "as clear of Jewish names as the register of an exclusive country club." In April 1933, the Toronto M.P., Sam Factor, asked a rhetorical question: "How many Jews are there in the high posts and on the boards of banks, trust companies, insurance firms, railroads and governments? Have we not men of ability? We can't get these positions because we are Jews."[8]

No doubt it was symptomatic of the problem of anti-semitism that a young Jewish psychology student, Esther Einbinder, decided to do her master's thesis in 1933 on "Attitudes towards Jews in Toronto." She found that businessmen and self-employed professionals were the most prejudiced against Jews. Thirty-five per cent of those interviewed from these groups wanted to exclude Jews from Canada, compared with 11 per cent of students, teachers and other salaried professionals. Prejudice sometimes verged on hysteria. One lawyer scribbled on his questionnaire: "I place a Jew on a lower plane than a sewer rat . . . they should be exterminated like vermin. But politics—Huh! Deport them—but where?"[9] (These findings in Einbinder's modest survey were verified by a pair of contemporary American investigators who went so far as to state that hostility towards the rising Jewish middle class predisposed their non-Jewish competitors to be pro-Nazi. "Over and over again," they wrote, "in casual conversation, business and professional men in the United States and Canada have disclosed their willingness to condone Hitler's destruction of constitutional liberties because his anti-semitic policy chimed in with their own antipathies.")[10]

Einbinder found dislike of Jews strong among university students. Although 45 per cent of those she polled admitted they had hardly known any Jews before coming to university, they shared their parents' prejudices. For instance, 80 per cent said they would not admit Jewish members to their clubs. The contagion of anti-semitism was well described by one girl. "When I first came to Varsity," she said, "a girl sat next to me in math class . . . . We talked, and walked home together . . . . I neither liked nor disliked her, until I found out she was Jewish. Then because Jewish students were so much disliked by other students I felt that she had been forward

. . . . The dislike may have been developed from the dislike of others for the Jews." Another of the student respondents unwittingly revealed a commonplace of the day that Jews (and other "foreigners") were not real citizens. He explained his antipathy in this manner: "In High School I ran up against a Jew who was clever enough to win all the scholarships, thus taking money from Canadians."

Considering the extent of prejudice, it is hardly surprising that acts of discrimination occurred. Predictably, Jews were most affected in their business dealings, home-buying, and recreation. Early in 1932 a Jewish member of the Ontario legislature, E. F. Singer, exposed the unfair practices of some insurance companies towards Jewish businessmen. Simply because of their race, they were treated as bad risks, and either paid higher premiums than non-Jewish clients or were refused insurance altogether. To end this kind of discrimination, Singer introduced an amendment to the Insurance Act. When the bill came up for second reading on March 22, all the members who debated it supported the principle that unfair discrimination against racial and religious groups should be stopped, but there was some attempt to quash the bill by questioning its practical value. Notwithstanding these last-ditch efforts, Premier George Henry's Conservative administration had the distinction of enacting the first piece of human rights legislation in Canada, when Ontario's Insurance Act was amended to read:

> Any licensed insurer which discriminates unfairly between risks within Ontario because of the race or religion of the insured shall be guilty of an offence.[11]

Overt discrimination in housing and recreation was blatant. Entire suburbs were closed to Jews, and restrictive covenants, prohibiting the sale of certain land or houses to Jewish buyers, were upheld in the courts. The city-owned Toronto Island was rented out to cottagers on twenty-one-year leases. On one part of the island "Gentiles Only" signs began to bloom in the summer of 1932. As it happened, the chairman of the Parks Commission was a Jewish alderman, J. J. Glass, and he managed to have a clause inserted in the leases, to the effect that signs could not be erected on city property without the commission's approval.[12] But the signs were like weeds. Eradicated in one area, they sprang up in another. Motorists driving into Toronto were greeted by a large "Gentiles Only" sign on a private beach just outside the city limits. Summer resorts displayed signs stating "No Jews or Dogs Allowed" and their owners distributed brochures assuring prospective guests that their clientele was restricted.

It was to rid the landscape of discriminatory signs that a modest human rights bill made a fleeting appearance in the Ontario legislature. Early in the 1933 session, a young Conservative backbencher, Argue Martin of Hamilton, introduced a bill to prohibit advertisements and notices which discriminated on the basis of race and religion. The proposed bill, vigorously seconded by Singer, had teeth in it, with provision for fines ranging from $50 to $500.

The liberal-minded *Toronto Daily Star* hailed the Martin bill as "a worthy measure." The columnist was the Reverend Salem Bland, who wrote under the *nom de plume* of "The Observer." Bland was a radical social reformer of the type of J. S. Woodsworth, the founder of the CCF party. He used his column in Canada's largest daily newspaper to support progressive causes such as collective bargaining and the CCF ("Canada's best hope"). The friend of racial and religious minorities, Bland agreed that discriminatory notices were "an unfair and oppressive situation." They hurt the feelings of a class of people and spread the infection of prejudice. Notices which excluded the Jewish people probably inflicted the greatest pain,

> just now when a once great and enlightened nation in Europe seems likely to give dictatorial power to a madman, who professes to be bent on reviving the hideous medieval persecution of the race that has laid the world under greater obligations than any other, and when in a neighbouring province there is going on a persistent attempt to kindle the same foul flame in Canada.[13]

The column is a resounding credo of liberalism, but one which clearly reveals the limits of even the most advanced contemporary thinking in the field of human rights. Although landlords, employers and resort owners might not advertise their restrictive practices, the Reverend Bland took it for granted that they were quite within their rights to discriminate on the basis of race or creed. Readers were assured that:

> The right of an employer to decline an applicant for any reason that seems good to him is not infringed by the bill, nor the right of hotel managers and of proprietors of apartment houses, office buildings, tourist stops, amusement places to refuse as tenants or visitors people deemed unwelcome or undesirable: the bill merely insists that such a refusal must be made as quietly as possible and not proclaimed to the world on a sign board, through circulars, or by way of broadcast or newspaper columns.*

If the "small-l" liberal press was ready for such a law, the Ontario legislature was not. Despite eloquent pleading from its sponsor, the Legal Bills committee threw it out. The chairman stated that while appreciating the point of view of the proponents of the bill, he doubted if it would accomplish the goal set for it. The most that the committee was prepared to do was to present a resolution to the House, strongly condemning the practices which Martin had sought to eradicate through his legislation.

The failure to ban "the publicly flaunted prejudice of the signboards"[14] was particularly disturbing to E. F. Singer, who feared that anti-semitism was spreading in Ontario. As a politician he had his ear to the ground, and it was already apparent to him that Hitler's propaganda was having an effect. "Unless something is done quickly," he warned a Zionist convention, "the Jewish people may well meet the same fate in Canada that the Jews are meeting in Germany . . . . No fire is so easily kindled as anti-semitism. The fire is dormant in Canada, it has not yet blazed up, but the spark is there. Germany is not the only place with prejudice. Look at Quebec."[15]

All Canadians were aware of what was happening in Germany. Nazi brutality was blazoned across the newspapers. The

---

*Even the bill's sponsors agreed with this point of view. In arguing for the bill, Martin pointed out that it did not interfere with private communications from hotels or resorts to the effect that certain races were barred: it would just prevent "gratuitous insults" in public. (*Toronto Star*, March 14, 1933).

Toronto Star sent Pierre Van Passen to Berlin to cover the unprecedented events of Hitler's dictatorship, and his eye-witness accounts of street violence, the official boycott of Jewish stores, and public degradation of Jewish citizens left nothing to the imagination. It has been pointed out that Hitler made no secret of his atrocities from the beginning. The lack of censorship, which seemed inexplicable at the time, was carefully calculated. It was based on the assumption that worldwide anti-semitism created a receptivity for persecution of the Jews, and that it was really favourable publicity for the New Germany. Unfortunately, in the disturbed world of the thirties, this did not prove an entire miscalculation. As a Canadian sociologist has pointed out, Hitler made the Jews appear "permissible targets of physical attack,"[16] thus bringing into the open hitherto latent anti-semitic aggression.

In Ontario, the first imitation of Hitler's tactics occurred in the summer of 1933 in Toronto's Balmy Beach area, described by a reporter of the day as "a residential section in the east end of the city with a mile and a half of boardwalk lined with attractive Gentile residences facing Lake Ontario and a wide beach."[17] Populated almost entirely by Britishers, Balmy Beach had the lowest percentage of ethnic population in the city. In such a homogeneous district, dislike of strangers may have been endemic; at any rate, the residents deeply resented the foreign-looking people who came from centre town to use the public beaches, accusing them of littering and of changing their clothes in the open.[18] Inspired by the example of the Nazis, some of the local youth began sporting swastika emblems, scrawling "Heil Hitler" over the boardwalk, and harassing Jewish bathers. Identifying themselves as members of a Swastika Club, they were soon embroiled in clashes with young Jews from outside the district, which put them on the front pages of the newspapers.

Opinion was divided on how seriously to take the Swastika Club which, by the first week of August, was claiming "three to four thousand sympathizers who have filled out membership applications."[19] Jewish leaders themselves were of two minds. Some held that the matter was receiving too much publicity, that there was no cause for worry since "people here are too broad-minded."[20] Others felt that the recent events marked the expansion into Ontario of the Quebec fascist movement. Non-Jewish liberals were also split. A spokesman for the United Church expressed great concern:

> It is unfortunate that the influence of Hitler should have gained a foothold in Canada. There is no room in this country for such pernicious doctrines as the Nazis are preaching. Unless this Swastika Club is nipped in the bud, I have grave fears that we may have a serious situation on our hands. I think the police should exert every effort to see that their sinister influence does not spread.[21]

On the other hand, the *Toronto Star*, while reproving the young "Swastikas," declared that there was "no anti-semite movement here." Nevertheless, just to make sure (and to make news), the *Star* wired Berlin to ask if there was "any foundation for rumours current here that anti-Jewish movement in Canada is allied with German Fascisti?"; to which Hitler's aide, "Putzi" Hanfstaengl replied: "Absurd to say Canadian anti-Jewish outbreaks in any way connected with Nazi movement here."[22]

How significant was the Swastika Club, and how broad a base did it operate from? Its members were teenage boys and young men in their early twenties; of the original thirty-five, all were of British origin. Although the club spokesman had inherited a German name from a grandfather, he too was of British ancestry and had come over from Scotland as a child of four. This young man, whose name was Bert, had studied at the University of Montreal for a short time, and may have picked up ideas from some of the pro-fascist students there. The headquarters of the Swastika Club was the back room of his candy store, and it was there that the badges with the swastika motif were sold. The only other identifiable leader was a good-looking youth about twenty whose surname was Mackay. Neither they nor their followers appear to have been hoodlums; they came from the middle class and had good connections in the neighbourhood. Indeed, they hinted at backing from the solid citizens of the Beaches, as for instance when Bert told a reporter that three prominent women were trying to form a ladies' auxilliary of the Swastika Club.[23]

Such community support was further indicated at a meeting at City Hall, called for the purpose of ending the tension in the East

End. Bert informed the mayor that "prominent residents" of the Beaches had come forward with an offer of moral and financial assistance for a larger organization to carry on the work started by the Swastika Club. The swastika emblem and the name were to be dropped and the new organization would be open to all residents regardless of nationality or creed. In effect, it was to be a citizen police, to "assist civic authorities to exclude from their district all obnoxious and undesirable elements that tend to destroy the natural beauty and property values of their residential district." Despite disturbing vigilante overtones, the mayor hurriedly endorsed the idea in the interests of peace, and arranged on the spot for police cooperation with the new organization.[24]

This successful negotiation nevertheless marked the end of Bert's ascendancy in his group. Evidently the swastika symbol was non-negotiable and, in giving it up, he lost the confidence of his fellows.[25] What happened then was that a more radical element of the Right took over and re-formed the Swastika Club. At the same time, like-minded groups began to surface, either dug out by the press or encouraged by the attention given to the Swastikas. One such group was a branch of the Steel Helmets, composed of about thirty German war veterans who met in a little restaurant on Jarvis Street. At least one of these was an admitted Nazi party member and it turned out that there was a nucleus Nazi group in the city. However, it was not Toronto but Kitchener, Ontario, that next made the headlines, with a Brownshirt party boasting a fascist and anti-semitic program.

Actually fascism in Kitchener was very much a one-man show, promoted by a forty-year-old German named Otto Becker who had come to Canada from Berlin in 1929. In 1933 he was out of work and living on relief. Not long before, he had tried to extort money from local Jews, allegedly to help their brethren in Germany. When next heard of, he was organizing a Swastika Club to be launched at a public meeting in Kitchener. In advance of the meeting, he printed and distributed a pamphlet sounding the communist alarm: "War declared against Marxism, Communism and Bolshevism. Canada's answer is 85,000 Fascists in Montreal on July 30, 1933. Real Canadian Fascists. 1,200 Swastikas in Toronto August 1, 1933. What about you, Kitchener and Waterloo?" Unlike the other Swastika Clubs, which were disingenuous about their anti-semitism,

Becker was candid. The pamphlet announced that no Jews would be admitted to the public meeting, and he himself used all the anti-semitic catch-phrases current in Germany in the 1920s. "It is my opinion," he told a reporter, "that anyone created by Heaven, no matter what his colour, race or creed, has the right to live, but he has no right to live on Christians without producing. It is his duty to work."[26] Strange words from an unnaturalized visitor who was living on welfare and cadging money under false pretences from the group he called parasites.

Printing literature and sponsoring a public meeting cost money. Who was subsidizing Becker? Funds may have come from some sympathizers among the Kitchener Germans, but it is also possible that Becker received money from Arcand or the *Fédération des Clubs Ouvriers*. When asked if he was working with the Montreal fascists he replied, "Yes we are, but I do not want to tell you too much about that yet."[27] Whether or not this was true, he had definitely contacted the Toronto Swastika Club because Mackay participated in his public meeting which was held on August 14, 1933.

This meeting was a fiasco. There was an overflow crowd, but they had come to jeer rather than to cheer the principals. Some were communists—the evening closed with a small group singing the Red Anthem—and others were Jews who defied Becker's pro-hibition; most of the audience, however, were solid burghers, Ger-man and non-German, who were there to protest the holding of a Nazi rally in their city. From the moment the brown-shirted Becker and Mackay opened the meeting with arms raised in the Nazi sa-lute, booing and heckling filled the hall. At every word against the Jews, the audience audibly expressed its displeasure. At one point a man jumped on the platform and began warning the people against "rotten Nazism." Fearing a riot, the police told Becker that they might have to use tear gas and advised him to close the meeting. He did so, defiantly shouting "Heil Hitler." Mackay, for his part, meekly removed his swastika badge when accosted by an irate Jew.[28]

The violent reaction to Becker's comic opera Nazi movement was no doubt communist-inspired in part. It does not wholly ex-plain, however, the hostile behaviour of the large audience. With 53 per cent of its population of German origin, Kitchener remained very sensitive throughout the thirties on the subject of Hitler. Unlike some German communities in the West, Kitchener Germans were careful to avoid any semblance of anti-semitism. Although there had been some boycotting of Jewish stores in April, at the time of the highly publicized Nazi boycott, the tiny Jewish community of 411 souls lived peacefully enough with the German majority. By and large, the Jews greeted Becker's Nazi talk with equanimity and the familiar reliance on (to quote one Jewish citizen) "British justice and fair play." Kitchener sealed its disapproval of Becker's short-lived Swastika Club with a resolution passed by the City Council:

> That this Council looks with disfavour upon any organization that among their aims and objectives brings oppression and discrimination upon any creed, and that they call upon all public servants, and citizens in general, to discourage and prevent as far as they are able the fostering of such an objective by any club, body or organization.[29]

Meanwhile word got around that Becker was to be deported at his own request. Thus Kitchener returned to normal.

But the Jewish incidents continued. The next to occur was in a park on the fringes of the largest Jewish district in Toronto.

On August 17 headlines in the *Toronto Star* announced "Six Hours of Rioting Follows Hitler Shout—Scores Hurt, Two Held." The riot had occurred at a baseball game between Jewish and non-Jewish teams in Willowvale Park in the working-class district known as Christie Pits. It started when someone waved a swastika flag and cries of "Heil Hitler" rang out. A fight began on the field and spread throughout the park. The quick appearance of makeshift weapons such as sledge hammers, lead pipe and sawed-off bats testify to the planning and organization behind the incident. The ten thousand spectators fell victim to mob psychology, surging about the park to get a better view of the fighting. With the arrival of truckloads of young Jews, the battle escalated. Outside the park, several Jewish pedestrians, oblivious of what was happening, were assaulted by roving gangs and badly beaten. The few police on hand were totally unequipped to control the riot. The extent of their intervention was to arrest two rioters for carrying weapons. Fighting did not cease until two o'clock in the morning.

This kind of public violence was too reminiscent of recent events in Nazi Germany to be taken lightly. The Willowvale riot was said to be the opening wedge of a fascist movement in Toronto. The *Star* proclaimed that "in violence and intensity of racial feeling [it was] one of the worst free-for-alls ever seen in this city."[30] The authorities were under pressure to act, the more so when it came out that the Chief of Police had been warned of the blow-up by the Parks Commission. But Chief Draper had chosen instead to deploy his available men at Allan Gardens, where a meeting of the Unemployed Ex-Servicemen's Association was scheduled.

Brigadier-General Draper was a perfect example of those in positions of wealth and power who believed that the political and economic system was being undermined by communists. He saw communists everywhere, and any protest group received his undivided attention. Outdoor meetings of the unemployed were broken up by a charge of mounted policemen or by a concentrated blast of exhaust fumes from a serried rank of police cars. The Hyde Park tradition was one British institution the Anglophiles of Toronto's establishment chose not to emulate. Draper was the prototype of the "law and order man." Liberal-minded contemporaries described his methods as "Cossackism," the *Windsor Star* going so far as to call his repression of free speech and free assembly "a national scandal." For refusing to provide adequate protection at Willowvale Park, Draper was, for once, criticized by his own Police Commission. "Why," he was asked, "can so many police be marshalled for suppression of Communists and not the Swastika Clubs?" Notwithstanding Draper's attitude, the city administration promised action against the Swastika Clubs. The mayor announced that they were under investigation by the police, and that persons wearing the swastika emblem would be liable to prosecution. Police immediately began rounding up the rioters and four arrests were made.

Those arrested were members of the Christie Pits gang, a group of about a hundred bored and unemployed youths who passed their time loitering around the park. Known as "the scourge of foreigners," all were of Anglo-Saxon parentage. It is evident that they were the instigators of the Willowvale riot. After it was over, they continued terrorizing Jews to the point that some elderly people were afraid to walk to the corner store. Other groups of youths followed the example of the Christie Pits gang, vacating their poolroom haunts for the amusement of driving people out of the city parks.[31] Were these youths the stuff of which fascists were made? It is doubtful. While chronic unemployment would have made them bitter and discontented, the gang structure itself gave them a sense of belonging that precluded the need for a fuehrer or an ideology. Far from the atomized masses identified by Hannah Arendt as potential fascists, these gangs were simply attracted by the Nazis' violence and brutality which fitted in with their own way of life. Their commitment to fascism or Nazism was very superficial. They had merely pre-empted the swastika as a licence for violence in the streets.

The real opposition to the Christie Pits gang in its new phase of activity did not come from the police but from some tough sons of Jewish immigrants employed in the garment industry on Spadina Avenue. It was these youths who had descended upon Willowvale Park the night of the riot. In their toughness, they were almost a prefiguration of the postwar Jews who founded the state of Israel. A spokesman for the group told a reporter that "rather than submit to the outrages that have been perpetrated on our race, we would die on the streets." They were no gang of rowdies, he said, but old schoolmates and co-workers in the clothing factories who had banded together to combat the Swastika Clubs. They rejected the role of victim and scapegoat, and he went on to explain the uncharacteristic militancy of these young Jewish Canadians.

> These boys are all British. They were brought up in Canadian schools and have learned something of the British bulldog idea never to give up without a fight. The teaching of passive resistance no longer carries any weight.[32]

Their stance is all the more remarkable in that their elders counselled patience, advising the youths against squad tactics and "taking the law into their own hands." Perhaps they would have had more confidence in the protection of the law if the four members of the Christie Pits gang, arrested for rioting, had not been freed because the magistrate regarded their swastikas as "all a joke."

Meanwhile a new adult association had been formed at the East End Beaches with the express purpose of "guarding the rights of Gentiles." An amalgamation of the Beaches Protective Association and a splinter group from the Swastika Club, the new organization called itself the Swastika Association of Canada and planned to spread from coast to coast. This marks the first public appearance of the man who was to be Ontario's number one fascist, Joseph C. Farr. A native of Northern Ireland, Farr had served in the British army as a sergeant-major. In Canada he was an active Orangeman. He was also extremely active in harassing Jews on the public beaches—an activity which distinguished his brand of fascism throughout the decade. Farr was first vice-president of the new association and introduced it to the public in a press interview. While giving the names of the executive (among them Mackay of the original Swastika Club), he withheld their addresses for security reasons. According to Farr, the primary aim was a campaign against "all those who through deceit or unscrupulous dealings would hinder in any way the advancement of Gentiles' rights in our own community." Although they had adopted the swastika, he insisted that they had no connection with Germany. He said they planned to hold a public meeting soon, "if we can get away with it," and a membership campaign was scheduled to begin the following week. Although the organization was the negation of human rights, Farr clothed it in virtues: "We are a purely Canadian organization to foster and encourage unselfishness, good fellowship, truth and loyalty to King and Country." The good fellowship included a program akin to the *achat chez nous* movement in Quebec. As Farr told the reporters, "We plan to promote a strong Gentile business appeal."[33]

V Western Fascists

In western Canada, Anglo-Saxon nativism was diluted by the vast number of immigrants from central and eastern Europe. In 1931 half the population of the prairies was of non-British and non-French origin. Dr. Walter Murray, then president of the University of Saskatchewan and a booster of minority rights, commented that in the eastern cities newcomers were greeted with ignorant jeers while out west they received a helping hand.[1] The West looked a good deal less like the mother country, too. In place of the red brick, Victorian gingerbread houses of the Ontario towns, there were Ukrainian villages of frame houses with outdoor clay ovens and poppies and sunflowers growing over wooden fences, and Mennonite communities with smoke houses and stacks of peat. Nevertheless, the West was also run by Anglo-Saxons, and ethnic groups struggled to be accepted by them and to conform to the dominant British culture. A young Ukrainian, speaking for his peers, remarked, "If we could ask for anything at all, it would be just to fit in."[2] And a twenty-five-year-old Jewish lawyer in Winnipeg expressed the same feeling when he said, "I don't ask anything except the opportunity to participate as an equal in the communal life of this country."[3]

It was a fact that western Jews met less discrimination than those in central Canada. For instance, the proportion of Jewish doctors and lawyers was twice as high in Winnipeg as in Toronto, and participation in the salaried professions was atypically on a par with the average for all origins, mainly because Jewish women teachers were hired by the public schools. This greater acceptability was attributable to the fact that education was at a premium where so high a proportion of the population was foreign-speaking. Canadian Jews were relatively well educated, with one of every 96 attending university, compared with a national average of one out of 316. Nonetheless, in 1934 a Jewish teacher brought what appears to have been a justified complaint of racial discrimination against the assistant superintendent of Winnipeg Public Schools and several principals.[4]

While Jews, along with other ethnic groups, may have met with greater tolerance in western Canada, many of the ethnic groups themselves were carriers of anti-semitism. Among their old country quarrels, they brought over the traditional peasant attitude towards the Jew—a deep-rooted folk antagonism that had manifested itself through the centuries in pogroms and ghettos. This created a receptivity among some ethnic groups for fascist propaganda which, by and large, was simply an attack upon the Jewish people. Moreover, the split in their ranks over the issue of communism made the east European communities a focus for fascist activity. For example, the Ukrainian community, which accounted for roughly 10 per cent of the population in the three prairie provinces, was seriously divided. Those who had emigrated during the Tsarist regime tended to be pro-communist, while those who came over during the twenties were mainly anti-communist because the Bolshevik Revolution had failed to produce an independent Ukraine. Among the latter were right-wing nationalists who continued their struggle for the liberation of their homeland, principally by fighting their pro-communist compatriots.[5] Their militant anti-communism, combined with a hereditary dislike of Jews, made them ready recruits for a fascist movement.

German-speaking Canadians were another natural target for fascist organizers. The largest ethnic group on the prairies, they formed 15 per cent of the population and in Saskatchewan alone numbered 129,000. They were, however, far removed from Germany. By the 1930s, 70 per cent of the German-Canadians were native-born, and of the foreign-born, only a small proportion had come from Germany: most were from eastern Europe where they had lived for centuries. Nationalism in the newly formed states had brought discrimination against the German minorities, and during the 1920s thousands had emigrated to Canada.

From the accession of Hitler, Nazi propaganda was directed overseas to Canada's half a million Germans. The principal agency was the *Auslandorganisation* (AO), the foreign division of the Nazi party. Directed by Ernest Bohle, the AO attempted to unite all Germans in foreign countries, regardless of citizenship. There was a North American "desk," and a special division for merchant seamen and sailors on German liners, who provided a network for Bohle's propaganda activities. Goebbel's Ministry of Propaganda also tailored material for the foreign market, and there were a number of private and semi-governmental agencies, such as the Fichte-Bund, in the field as well.[6]

Officially, the Nazis denied any activity among Germans abroad. This was stated vehemently by the German consuls general in Montreal and Winnipeg. In particular, they insisted that Nazi anti-semitism was for domestic use only and not for export.[7] Of course this was untrue; Hitler regarded Germans everywhere as citizens of the Reich, bound by ties of blood. In his memoirs Herman Rauschning, a high official at the beginning of the Nazi regime, portrays Hitler instructing a conference of overseas Nazi leaders to set up two German societies in every country: one to talk loyalty to the adopted land and the other to act as a revolutionary agency in the interests of Germany. In encouraging subversion, the Fuehrer made no distinction between citizens of Germany and Germans who were citizens of other countries.

The Nazi agency used to infiltrate German communities in North America was the Friends of the New Germany, later to become the German-American Bund under Fritz Kuhn of Detroit. In the spring of 1933 an agent was assigned to organize Canadian branches of the Friends, and by chance his correspondence with a German resident of Winnipeg fell into the hands of a local Jewish lawyer, Max Finkelstein. Writing from Detroit, this agent, Hans Strauss, explained to his Winnipeg contact that "Canada will be a territory of its own and I will organize there the branches." His letter apparently was favourably received because in his next, Strauss wrote:

> I certainly appreciate your and your fellow compatriots interest in Hitler and his ideas and ideals. So do we appreciate your willingness to cooperate with us in establishing Nazi groups and locals throughout Canada.[8]

One of Winnipeg's distinguished citizens, Finkelstein was not only a Jewish communal leader but an outstanding lawyer whose court victories included a famous extradition case against the Tsar.[9] He was hardly the man to be taken in by a hoax or forgery. Alarmed by the revelations in the Strauss letters, he forwarded them to S. W. Jacobs, who, in hopes of having Strauss stopped at the border, quickly wrote to the Secretary of State, C. H. Cahan, Commissioner MacBrien of the RCMP, and the Minister of Immigration, W. A. Gordon.[10] Whether or not Strauss entered the country in 1933, other Nazi agents certainly came in from time to time.

More effective than these surreptitious visitors were the shiploads of propaganda sent over from Germany. Despite their denials, the consuls were the main distributors. Early in 1934 Jacobs raised the matter in the House of Commons. He stated that publications "grossly offensive to Jews . . . and likely to stir up enmity and strife in this country against the Jews" were being issued from the German consulate in Montreal, and he asked the Minister of Justice, H. A. Guthrie, whether the consul general, Dr. Kempf, would be removed. Guthrie replied that he saw "no occasion" for the withdrawal of Dr. Kempf, adding that the Canadian government had always got along well with him. Nevertheless, Jacobs' question sparked a public response which confirmed that German propaganda was being widely distributed, especially in the West. A woman from Vegreville, Alberta, sent the government some samples that were in circulation there. These included articles from the Fichte-Bund and a reprint of a column by Lord Rothermere, praising Mussolini and Hitler extravagantly.[11] During 1933 and well into 1934 Rothermere's *Daily Mail* was at the service of Sir Oswald Mosley and indirectly of the fascist dictators. The English press lord himself contributed a few encomiums, such as this one entitled "Youth Triumphant," in which he compared Hitler's Germany to Elizabethan England. Understandably, the Nazi propaganda mill made good use of it. The Rothermere article also turned up in the Mennonite town of Winkler, Manitoba, and among the Winnipeg German community.[12]

Of German Canadians, the Mennonites were particularly receptive to Hitler, largely because they approved of his vociferous anti-communism. According to a Canadian Mennonite scholar, "It is a well-known fact that strong pro-Nazi sentiments were expressed in the Mennonite press in the thirties."[13] But even among those Mennonites with Nazi leanings, their traditional pacifism created an ambivalence towards Hitler's militaristic regime. They were not the stuff that revolutionaries of the Right were made of. A different breed were the young men who emigrated from Germany after the war. They brought with them the same bitterness that had given birth to the Nazi movement. Some had been members of the Freikorps, and as a group they tended to be ultra right-wing. Indeed, the whole postwar wave was "considered by prewar settlers to be sympathetic to the Nazis."[14] But even some highly assimilated Germans, in Canada for many years, were not immune to stirrings of national pride in the newly revitalized fatherland after 1933.[15]

Considering the ferment of anti-communism and anti-semitism among some European settlers, it is hardly surprising that when a fascist group formed in Winnipeg in 1933 it drew strength from the foreign element. But it was not the Ukrainian nationalists or the postwar German immigrants who started the movement or provided the leadership. The founders were Anglo-Saxon ex-soldiers. The correlation between militarism and fascism is well documented. Kurt Ludecke, a witness of the rise of fascism, observed that "in Germany and Italy the offensive power of the fascist groups had originally come almost entirely from the veterans' organizations, the old front-line fighters."[16] And so it was in Winnipeg where a dozen veterans, with an old British soldier at their head, launched the brown-shirted Canadian Nationalist Party at a public meeting on September 26, 1933.

The focal figure was William Whittaker, an Englishman in his late fifties. As a young man he had fought in three imperialist campaigns and travelled throughout the empire. Since coming to Canada twenty-eight years before, he had worked as a lumberjack and a policeman; he was always careful to explain that he had been too old to fight in the Great War.[17] Whittaker and his assistant, a nineteen-year-old named Jack Cole, wore khaki shirts, light brown breeches and riding boots. Shrugging off the obvious resemblance to storm troopers as coincidental, they maintained that their costumes were "typically Western Canadian dress."

The new party assumed a posture of fervent patriotism. The meeting hall was decorated with Union Jacks and in his opening remarks, Whittaker pledged the party's loyalty to the crown. Their objective, he announced, was to fight communism "tooth and nail" and to end the Depression: to attain these ends the party would shortly enter national politics. The main plank in the Nationalist platform was the abolition of provincial legislatures. "With one national government we could stop communism," Whittaker asserted, "but with so many governments it has a better chance to flourish and become a dangerous menace to law and order in this country." Once centralized, Canada under the Nationalist Party would become a corporate state, but Whittaker did not dwell on the intricacies of corporatism. He simply promised to introduce a new economic system "by peaceful means," which would raise the living standards of the masses. Young Cole's role was to make an appeal to youth with promises of "fair opportunity"; many young men in 1933 had been without work since leaving school. Not a word was said against the Jews; in fact, Whittaker insisted that the party was not affiliated with fascist organizations in eastern Canada. None of which stopped a local communist from informing the over-credulous that the Nationalist Party were "fascists in disguise."

The truth of this was apparent when the party began publishing a virulently anti-semitic monthly called *The Canadian Nationalist.* Edited by Whittaker, it was printed by the publisher of a Mennonite church paper, Herman Neufeld; in his own paper, Neufeld praised Hitler, excerpted speeches by Goebbels, and promoted Nazism among the Mennonite flock.[18] *The Canadian Nationalist* reprinted all the staples of mythic anti-semitism, including the spurious Protocols. And at Nationalist meetings, which were increasing in attendance and spreading to towns outside Winnipeg, speakers denounced the Jews and equated them with communists. They also played upon the economic distress of their listeners with tirades against "international finance." Despite the party's open anti-semitism, Whittaker unabashedly denied charges of racial hatred.

It was frankly a shirt movement now, with khaki-clad stewards pacing the aisles and guarding the doors. Some of the party's "brass" wore swastika tie-pins with their uniforms. The original leadership, described by Whittaker as a dozen veterans, had put the stamp of militarism on the party, and the example of Germany's Nazis did the rest. Suspicions aroused by the party's paramilitary character were confirmed when a police raid of Nationalist headquarters yielded lists of members classified by fighting skills—for example, ability to handle rifles or fly aircraft. Veterans continued to be much in evidence at the public meetings. The ultra-patriotic speeches, delivered against a backdrop of the Union Jack, and the barrackroom camaraderie were calculated to appeal to old soldiers who had fought with the Canadian Expeditionary Force, and now languished, many of them unemployed, in the dreary days of the Depression.

But the movement's greatest appeal was to the European immigrant groups. The astute Whittaker held many meetings in the ethnic districts of North Winnipeg and in the Mennonite towns of the hinterland. While the leadership remained Anglo-Saxon except for two Mennonite names, the rank and file were largely European immigrants. During a clash with anti-fascists in June 1934, the list of injured Brownshirts was almost entirely non-British.[19] (The involvement of a number of Mennonites caused a controversy within that community since traditionalists were aghast at this abandonment of the non-resistance position.)[20] Like the officer corps of Anglo-Saxons, the ethnic recruits wore the brown shirt of the movement.

The formation of a fascist organization was parallelled by the massing of anti-fascist forces. Fiery Reds from the ethnic districts, blue-collar British-born communists and young militant Jews began appearing at Nationalist meetings, which now bristled with uniformed Brownshirts. Several police officers always dotted the hall as well. The presence of the police gave Whittaker, himself an ex-policeman, psychological advantages over his adversaries. It not only protected his freedom of speech; when anti-fascist groups appeared and were headed off by Brownshirts and policemen together, it gave the impression of an alliance between the two. This did not deter the visitors from attempting to break up the meetings, and sometimes the RCMP had to be called in to help restore law and order.

Organized labour was the first to raise a public outcry against the fascists in Winnipeg. Bearing in mind recent events in Germany, union members saw the initial attack on the Jews spreading to an attack on the labour movement. In February 1934, the Trades and Labour Congress resolved to investigate the Nationalist Party, in particular its sources of financial support (rumoured to come from public men behind the scenes). At the same time, John

Queen, the leader of the Independent Labour Party, raised the matter in the legislature. Queen was a hero of the labour movement. One of the men imprisoned for seditious conspiracy following the Winnipeg general strike, his communist sympathies did not hinder him from repeated election to public office—as alderman, MLA, and in 1935 mayor of Winnipeg.

On February 13, 1934, Queen made front-page news when he charged in the legislature that Winnipeg's fascists were anti-semitic and aimed at the overthrow of constitutional government. Citing "growing sentiment for dictatorship even in Canada," he told the House that although he believed in free speech, the fascist organization should obviously be suppressed. Canada was a land of mixed nationalities that so far had mingled together with little disturbance, but now a group had arisen to stir up racial feelings. That sort of movement should not be tolerated. He criticized the Attorney General, W. J. Major, for taking no action when the police uncovered evidence of "seditious conspiracy" at Nationalist Party headquarters. Was this flaunting of constitutional authority to be allowed to continue, especially since the fascist movement was threatening to organize on a dominion-wide basis? Waving an issue of *The Canadian Nationalist* before the House, Queen offered it as proof that the fascists were receiving financing from somewhere as yet unknown. In Queen's view, the Nationalist Party "made little appeal to British minds, but to certain European minds in the population, its anti-Jewish trend appealed."[21]

The Attorney General's initial response to this challenge was playful. He was glad to know, he said, that Mr. Queen was for law and order and would never throw a bomb for Karl Marx. Major soon realized, however, that the notoriety of the fascist movement could become a political issue if not handled carefully. Accordingly, he pushed Queen off the front pages with a strong statement of government policy regarding "agitators, both communists and those who profess to be ultra-nationalists." Beginning with the familiar tribute to the immigrants' "gifts" which they brought to their adopted country, he proceeded to read a lesson to the ethnic population:

> Equality before the law of all citizens whatever their race or religion is a fundamental of those free institutions. The law

knows no distinction whether he be black or white, Nordic or Slav, Jew or Gentile. This is the foundation of our national life. There is no room for old discords and hates of the old lands of Europe. Our citizenship entails obligation to respect and accept the laws and rights of other citizens.

Then the Attorney General fell into the same trap as other lawyers and judges when he assumed that the Criminal Code covered group libel.

Whoever foments discord and hate between any sections of His Majesty's subjects is not only unworthy of citizenship but a law-breaker as well. He is guilty of seditious conspiracy and punishable as by statute provided.

Law and order would be maintained, he declared, and the authorities stood ready to deal with agitators. He advised law-abiding citizens to resist any attempt of agitators to secure members in an organization which, "while basing its objects on patriotism and loyalty, has as its real purpose the creating of racial strife and hatred against sections of our citizens."[22]

The next day the Attorney General was called upon to make good his words. The fascists had hastily arranged a meeting for that evening in a Ukrainian hall; it would almost certainly provoke a confrontation with the communists and other anti-fascists. Having committed himself to take action to maintain law and order, Major summoned the Ukrainians in charge of the hall to the legislature that afternoon and obtained their promise not to permit the meeting. By eight o'clock in the evening, a crowd of a thousand friends and foes had arrived at the hall to find closed doors guarded by "sturdy fur-coated members of the city police." Then Whittaker drove up and, calmly ignoring taunts of "Here comes Hitler," advised his followers to disperse quietly. The non-event made banner headlines: "Nationalist Meeting is Banned—Major, Fearing Clash of Communists and 'Brown Shirts', Stops Gathering."[23] Whittaker found himself in a strong position. If his fascists could not meet, neither should their rivals. On hearing that the communists were planning a meeting, he and some of his lieutenants called upon Major to stop it. According to Whittaker, the discussion was unproductive, but he used the occasion to expound Nationalist doctrines to the

Attorney General so he could later publicly boast of it. Eventually, the Nationalists convinced the mayor of Winnipeg to prevent the communist meeting.

The Attorney General was now confronted with a "rather thorny" problem, in the words of the *Winnipeg Free Press*: "He is to decide whether free speech should be unlimited or curtailed at the point where there is a strong possibility it will result in the cracking of heads."[24] To be the seeming opponent of freedom of speech was an unenviable position. Even the Toronto police were finally going to cease interfering with public meetings unless the law was actually broken.[25] Was Winnipeg to assume all the criticism that the liberal press had previously heaped upon Toronto? This was Major's dilemma. Furthermore, he must have realized by now that existing legislation gave no protection against defamation of a racial or religious group. So Whittaker was free to continue his anti-semitic propaganda and his denunciation of provincial governments, all in the name of freedom of speech and of assembly. The Nationalist meetings were allowed to resume; they attracted capacity crowds, and Whittaker used his platform to taunt the Attorney General. Speaking at Scandinavian Hall, he sneered that if the government had any grounds for suppressing his paper, they would have done so long ago.

By this time the racial slanders in *The Canadian Nationalist* had become so offensive that a Jewish MLA, Marcus Hyman, decided to sponsor legislation to curb what he labelled "the filthy and scurrilous publication of these racketeers." It was becoming increasingly difficult, he told the House, "to restrain some of our younger men from demonstrating their enraged resentment of these foul libels propagated against my people." To avoid violence, he proposed to introduce a bill prohibiting group libel, and on March 20, 1934, he duly did so. Although Hyman, who sat as an Independent Labour member, lacked the apparent advantage of belonging to the party in power, his bill won government support. The explanation is that the Bracken administration was also suffering from Whittaker's attacks. The Nationalists were undermining its authority; not only did their platform call for the abolition of provincial governments, but they were challenging the Attorney General. Without group libel legislation, Major could not back up his "warning to agitators" speech of February 20. Enlightened self-interest explains why the Bracken government passed the Hyman bill.

The Manitoba Defamation Act was the first and, until 1970, the only group libel law in Canada. It allowed any member of a racial or religious group that was being defamed to sue for an injunction against the publisher or author. The plaintiff did not have to prove that he was personally affected; it was sufficient cause if the published statements were "likely to expose" his race or religion to "hatred, contempt or ridicule, and tended to raise unrest and disorder among people." If convicted, the defendants would be ordered to permanently cease publication of the libels.[26] Concurrently, Hyman steered through an amendment to the Newspaper Act whereby the publisher's name was mandatory on all pamphlets and handbills. This was a measure intended to prevent convicted publishers and editors from setting up shop again under a different name.

Meanwhile, trouble between the fascists and the communist-led anti-fascists was steadily building up. On June 5, 1934, it erupted in a riot at Market Square, luridly described by the *Free Press*:

> Knives flashed in the fast-waning sunlight, heavy clubs crashed against cap-protected skulls, and huge slabs of wood were torn from the stalls of the market gardeners and used as battering rams against the tightly pressing wall of snarling humanity.

The "blood speckled" Nationalists got the worst of it. Managing to break away at last, they were rescued by a truck and whisked away to safety. About a dozen had to be taken to hospital.

The next day nine Brownshirts appeared in city police court, with bandaged heads and "natty brown uniforms spattered with stains." Seven were charged with taking part in an affray, but were released on bail of $1,000 each, although where the $7,000 came from is an unanswered question. The riot was said to be the worst civic disturbance since the 1919 strike. Whittaker used the broken skulls of his ethnic followers to proclaim it "the first battle in the cause of Gentile economic freedom," and he denounced the authorities for not taking action against the communists.[27] He claimed to have shown Premier Bracken evidence of a communist conspiracy.

There are indications that the riot may have been triggered from Moscow. It cannot have been coincidental that, almost to the day, violent anti-fascist disorders erupted in England, France and Canada. In France meetings of the right-wing *Croix de Feu* were broken up by local communists. In London, a mass meeting of Mosley's Blackshirts at Olympia Hall was invaded by a communist-led contingent. Both sides had clubs, and hundreds were injured in the fight. An American historian of Mosley's movement dates its decline from this riot, which shocked the British public with its violence.[28]

The Olympia riot coincided with Hitler's purge of Ernst Roehm and other Storm Trooper leaders. Canadian newspapers were filled with stories of the bloodshed. An outraged *Winnipeg Free Press* declared that the true nature of fascism stood revealed. The combination of events even caused that liberal organ to have second thoughts about unlimited freedom of speech. Speaking of police inaction at Mosley's meetings, the *Free Press* commented:

> So boundless is English zeal for free speech that the London police do not attend "private" meetings staged by any political group, no matter how great chances of violence seem to be, except on the invitation of the promoters.

Then followed a vivid description of the Blackshirts punching and kicking hecklers, wielding razor blades and brass knuckles—"and this happened in England, the motherland of democracy." No wonder some of the English papers were now asking if tolerance of free speech meant tolerance of organized brutality. The *Free Press* saw a message for Canadians in all this:

> Those who are attracted by the fascist idea, and there are some in Canada, should meditate on the implications of Fascist government as revealed by Hitler's outburst and, in less startling way, by the episode of the blackshirt meetings in London. Government by physical terrorism means a breakdown of civilized life.[29]

Such hard-hitting, anti-Nazi editorials brought down upon the *Free Press* the wrath of the German consul, Dr. Seelheim, and of many of the fifteen thousand Germans living in Winnipeg. To this the paper replied unrepentantly:

> Propaganda in defence of Nazism has everywhere abounded

recently. Newspapers have been flooded with letters. "Professors" real or bogus have toured the country making stereotyped speeches to audiences willing to listen. The yearly routine expenditure by Dr. Goebbels for propaganda purposes outside Germany is ten million pounds . . . [30]

In fact a Nazi agent was at work among the German Canadians. Dr. Karl (or Emil) Gerhardt, an erudite and urbane German who "dressed like Bond Street," had been assigned to start a Nazi organization which went by the name of the German League or Deutsche Bund. While masquerading as a purely cultural organization, its real purpose was to spread the Nazi propaganda line in Canada. Gerhardt began operations among the Ontario Germans of Kitchener and Waterloo, but early in September 1934 he was in Winnipeg, addressing German groups and soliciting members for the Bund.[31] Here was the "professor" referred to by the *Free Press*, and it would appear that he was indeed "bogus." A month later he was living in Montreal and posing as a McGill professor when a curious young medical student at his boarding house discovered that he was neither known nor employed by the university. Meanwhile Gerhardt lived very well in a three-room suite, where he held meetings and showed films to German visitors. The young medical student observed that the gatherings frequently included the German consul, Dr. Kempf. He also noted that his fellow boarder received mail from all over Canada.[32]

Another key person in the formation of the Bund was Bernard Bott, a German national who edited a pro-Hitler, anti-semitic paper in Regina, *Der Courier*. Evidently a paid agent of the Nazi propaganda organization, he returned to Germany periodically, on one visit receiving a medal for his Canadian services. In the autumn of 1934 he was transferred to Winnipeg, ostensibly to represent the German press in Canada but really to start the Deutsche Bund's official organ, the *Deutsche Zeitung*. His bosom friend was the German consul in Winnipeg, Dr. Seelheim, later to be revealed as the largest single shareholder of the paper, thus proving a direct tie-up between German government officials and Nazi propaganda in Canada.[33] It is also worth noting that, from its inception in 1935, the *Deutsche Zeitung* was printed by Herman Neufeld, the printer of Whittaker's hate sheet.

The Bund made its greatest headway in Winnipeg. James Gray, in his chronicle of the Depression years on the prairies, asserts that Nazis infiltrated the university, the schools and the churches. "Until the outbreak of war," he writes in *The Winter Years*, "anti-Nazism was a lost cause in Winnipeg and the boisterous rejection of appeasement by the *Free Press* won it few plaudits."[34] A strong allegation, but at the time of the Bund's inception a professor from Brandon University was on the lecture circuit, giving western Canadian service clubs his extremely pro-Hitler "Impressions of Berlin."

Nazi propaganda in Winnipeg reinforced Whittaker's efforts. Despite the anti-defamation legislation of March 1934, he continued to print libels against the Jewish people in *The Canadian Nationalist*. These reached epic proportions in the autumn with an article alleging that Canadian Jews practised ritual murder. Since this slander sheet enjoyed a wide circulation in the province and was sold openly on Winnipeg streets, a Jewish lawyer and former MLA decided to take court action. Captain W. V. Tobias, a war hero who had been decorated with the Military Cross, had the necessary prestige to champion a minority cause. Invoking the new legislation, he sued Whittaker and his printer, Herman Neufeld, for false and malicious libel. The case was heard in the Manitoba Court of King's Bench in February 1935 by Mr. Justice Percival Montague, who found the defendants guilty and issued an order perpetually restraining them from further publication of such libels against the Jewish race. He also awarded $300 in costs to the plaintiff.

The successful outcome of the Tobias case was a source of pride to many Manitobans. The conservative *Winnipeg Tribune* praised the judgment and thoughtfully assessed the legislation.

> Appeals to race prejudice, always harmful and despicable, are particularly out of place in Canada. They are difficult to deal with in law, because democracy calls for the utmost freedom in discussion of public issues, and anything that tends to hamper full political discussion is to be avoided. But this extension of the libel law is in no sense a gag on debate.

Nevertheless, it was far from a death blow for the western fascists. Whittaker and Arcand had formed a loose league the previous autumn and hints of a national campaign issued from both camps. Unlike Arcand, Whittaker played no significant part in the 1935 election; but like his Quebec counterpart he favoured R. B. Bennett. In the summer of 1935, the prime minister's harsh treatment of the "Trekkers" (the unemployed young men from the government labour camps) elicited Whittaker's congratulations. Among the Bennett Papers is this letter dated June 24, 1935:

> We, the members of the Canadian Nationalist Party, take this opportunity to congratulate the Premier of Canada for the firm stand he has taken, in dealing with the Communist leaders of the pseudo camp strikers who would dare to beard the British lion in his den at Ottawa. We still believe in the good advice of one of our great Empire leaders—"Fear God, Honour the King and keep your powder dry."

VI Mosleyites in Canada

In the summer of 1934 Winnipeg was the birthplace of yet another fascist movement, this one an attempt to import Mosley's Blackshirts. Indeed, its founders claimed that it was a branch of the British Union of Fascists and that there were similar branches in Australia, South Africa and New Zealand.[1] Did Sir Oswald actually launch an imperial movement? Or was the British Empire Union of Fascists (as it initially called itself in Winnipeg) the work of opportunists attaching themselves to his coattails? In any event, an uninspiring individual named Hubert Cox was in Winnipeg in June 1934 claiming to be Mosley's representative. The local leader was a former Whittaker lieutenant, Howard Simpkin, who had earlier led a splinter group away from the Canadian Nationalist Party. Understandably anxious to establish a separate identity for the new organization, Simpkin objected strenuously to the term "fascist" being applied to the Nationalists. He further disassociated himself and his organization from the anti-semitism of Whittaker's party, declaring that "anti-semitism was a symptom of Germany not of Fascism."[2]

With this advance publicity the British Empire Union of Fascists managed to attract about two hundred people to its inaugural meeting on June 28. Quite different from Whittaker's audiences, they were "a collection of perfectly good family men"[3] in search of a panacea that would pull the country out of the Depression. Many Canadians felt the old-line parties had let them down. To some extent, the parliamentary system was in disrepute in Canada as in other western democracies. While this tendency should not be exaggerated—Canada like Great Britain having a firmly entrenched parliamentary tradition nevertheless faith in the system was badly shaken by the Depression and the inadequacy of the government to alleviate the people's suffering. Disillusionment with the democratic process was only too understandable at the time. James Gray has described at first-hand the Depression years in Winnipeg, when middle-class heads of family, fallen from their formerly self-sufficient and self-respecting status, lined up for the dole. Unemployment and the fear of it ensured an audience of several hundred for Cox and Simpkin.

Cox opened the meeting with an outline of the principles and policies of the British fascists. Wearing the regulation black shirt and tie, he was a funereal rather than a martial figure. And his appearance was in keeping with his fashion of speech-making, which consisted mainly of reading aloud "in dismal tones" from a Mosley pamphlet. Delivered in such a lugubrious manner, his definition of fascism as "a spontaneous, international uprising against tyranny, exploitation, incompetence, avarice and retrogression" would hardly have roused enthusiasm in his listeners. Obviously Cox was not one of the great leaders whom, he told his audience, fascism had produced. The new party followed the Mosley line to the letter: it stood for "fascism by peaceful, legal and constitutional means," establishment of the corporate state, drastic economic change, a self-sufficient empire whose symbiotic nature would end the struggle for markets ("the chief cause of war"); anti-communism was, of course, a basic tenet. Cox reiterated that anti-semitism would form no part of Canadian fascist policy, emphasizing that it was condemned by Mosley. This was true for the moment only. Although Mosley had hitherto rejected "racial and religious persecution as alien to the British character,"[4] he was about to turn to it as a desperate expedient now that his star was waning. The Canadian branch of the Union of Fascists would obediently follow him into a policy of anti-semitism in the near future.

The meeting was then taken over by Simpkin. A proponent of the leadership principle, he asked rhetorically, "Who will be the Sir Oswald Mosley of Canada?" It was a question his weakly led organization would be asking until its final hours. Certainly Simpkin did not claim to have the necessary qualifications, although he recognized a constituency of his own in the veterans. "Them boys would stand by me," he was quoted as saying. The next speaker was a woman secretary who read out the party platform in greater detail. Her prepared text elaborated on the proposed political and economic system: parliament's role was to be that of an advisory body to the head of state; all citizens of the corporate state would be shareholders; a sliding scale of child allowances would be provided for all parents. The idea of common and preferred shares in the state caused some wrinkled brows and Simpkin interrupted the secretary to caution that fascism was not simple, it had taken him years to understand. When a member of the audience asked whether actuaries had been consulted on sources of revenue for the plan, Simpkin sidestepped. "Look at what governments cost, what about distributing that money?" he countered, adding "and there are the natural resources too." At this a voice from somewhere in the hall intoned sarcastically, "Flowing with milk and honey!" and at every reference to the social credit type of scheme, the disembodied voice repeated the remark, to Simpkin's evident consternation. The audience had a number of Doubting Thomases. One man called fascism the last stage of capitalism, while another brushed aside Simpkin's longings for a leader with a sneer: "Lead you into the wilderness, like as not." The *Free Press* reporter observed that, faced with embarrassing or difficult questions, Simpkin "hitches his trousers, stiffens his pompadour and declines to answer."[5] Despite cynical questions and inadequate answers, however, these middle-class people, fallen on hard times, had come out in the sincere hope that the new movement would have something to offer them. The hardships of the Depression were causing them to wander off democratic pathways.

As with Mosley's movement, the cornerstone of the Union of Fascists' policy was corporatism, the coercive state doctrine evolved by Mussolini. A form of representative government based on occupation, corporatism was something like a meeting of craft unions and employer organizations, supervised by government officials. Unlike the traditional parliamentary system, representatives were not elected by popular vote but selected by the government, according to rigidly maintained proportions of economic classes. This medieval schema, ordained from on high, purported to give the working classes the opportunity to express their will and consequently strikes were declared illegal. But, in effect, corporatism in Italy simply preserved the capitalistic status quo because the Italian farmers and workers started from too low a power base to speak as equals to the landowners and industrialists. Real power, however, rested with the state, which controlled both sides through its function of compulsory arbitration. Indeed, in every aspect of life, the state, in the person of Il Duce, was the supreme arbiter. Like all fascist movements, the Union of Fascists was content to keep free enterprise. Its platform stated that "Canadian Fascists believe in the maintenance of private ownership on as widely diffused a basis as possible, public and private initiative being co-ordinated through the Corporate State. "[6]

Under the name of the Canadian Union of Fascists (the imperial identification was dropped shortly after the first meeting), Simpkin's movement trickled out across the country. Within a year or so there were branches at Transcona in Manitoba, Toronto and Woodstock in Ontario, Regina and Vancouver.[7] The movement boasted of its affiliation with Mosley's British Union of Fascists and, to highlight the connection, its members wore black shirts. Its party organ, *The Thunderbolt,* printed in Toronto, carried advertisements for Mosley's *Action* and *The Blackshirt,* and reviewed books by British fascists. *The Thunderbolt's* editor was a young man named Charles Brandel (alias C.B. Crate), who represented the CUF at public meetings like the Youth Congress of May 1935. Eventually, Brandel replaced Simpkin as the leader of the CUF.

The CUF's western organizer was a Dr. R. Muir Johnstone of Vidora, Saskatchewan. An inveterate writer of letters to the editor, he was regarded as one of the many crackpots who offered the public their own versions of economic salvation.[8] Johnstone's gospel was corporatism, and it was this which ultimately brought him to the Mosleyites. He had previously been associated with a Toronto-based shirt organization grandly calling itself the Dominion State Party, and it was his aim to incorporate all the little local fascist groups in western Canada into this organization. Despite his grandiose plans, the Dominion State Party or "Whiteshirts" would not be worth mentioning except for the fact that they demonstrate a link between the Canadian and American fascist movements. According to Johnstone, they were affiliated with William Pelley's Silvershirts in the United States. Pelley, a writer on psychic and spiritualistic phenomena, founded the Nazi-inspired Silver Legion in

1933 and, in the hope of conquering the Bible Belt, was now organizing a second group under the name of the Christian Party. The Silvershirts never amounted to much; but in the dust bowl of Oklahoma in the mid-thirties, Pelley attracted attention and some support. Obviously Johnstone hoped that similar conditions in Saskatchewan would favour his movement. In particular, he expected northeast Saskatchewan, with its heavy German population, to be an easy target for organized fascism.[9]

To carry out his plans, Johnstone approached Simpkin and others in the CUF. Writing to Tom King of Moose Jaw in 1934, he said, "I am arranging to get fighting support funds from the Mosley group. His party will finance trustworthy workers for Western Canada on my recommendation." The result of these negotiations was that Johnstone joined the CUF. This change of loyalties cannot have been much of a wrench. A difference of opinion had already arisen between Johnstone and the pro-Hitler Toronto group. Although "a staunch believer in the Protocols [of Zion] and in the necessity of a fascist dictatorship in Canada" (as one Regina Jew remarked of him),[10] Johnstone was not a great admirer of Hitler's. Mosley was his model fascist and, so far as he understood them, he adopted Mosley's theories. Moreover, the CUF provided him with an outlet for his writing urge, and he became a frequent contributor to *The Thunderbolt*.[11]

Johnstone was violently opposed to socialism in any form, and he found himself fighting for souls with the new CCF party; indeed, there was considerable crossing of the line between the socialists and the fascists. When Tom King (an individual of his own ilk who also dabbled in monetary reform) deserted to the CCF, Johnstone used every argument to recall him to the fascist fold, among other things recommending that he read Mosley's *Greater Britain.* But this defection was offset by recent converts like the "cultured Dane" who left the CCF and, to Johnstone's gratification, became "a Silvershirt enthusiast and fascist."[12]

He made considerable efforts to expand into Alberta. When Aberhart swept into power in the summer of 1935, Johnstone made overtures to the Social Credit party on behalf of the CUF. He found, however, that there was insufficient common ground. In Johnstone's view, Social Credit would not work because it did not install the corporate state and fascist economics; according to him, Aberhart and his mentor, Major Douglas, did not recognize their real friends—the fascists.[13] *The Thunderbolt's* editor, Charles Brandel, also blamed Social Credit's imperfect fascism on Aberhart. "Abie," he wrote a correspondent in Alberta, "is too full of the milk of human kindness to catch the nearest way." Aberhart (when all was said and done) still fitted into the system of parliamentary democracy.

While Dr. Johnstone was wrestling with the inadequacies of Social Credit, Simpkin was looking eastward. To gain a foothold in Montreal, he opened negotiations with the *Fédération des Clubs Ouvriers*[14] which had not yet been completely displaced as Quebec's fascist movement by Arcand's National Social Christian Party. It is interesting that Arcand's own analysis of the *Fédération's* membership in 1933 bears a marked resemblance to Simpkin's "collection of perfectly good family men." According to Arcand (who hoped to bring them into *his* fold), they were "good, honest *pères de famille,* the unemployed who seek a ray of hope, working men who dream of improving their lot, responsible citizens who hope to make conditions in their homes a little happier."[15] These were not the discontented youths who personified his own movement.

But it was not only the "little man" who was attracted to Mussolini's ideas. Big business was also tempted by the thought of a union or coalition government with dictatorial powers that could throw out poor cabinet ministers and introduce strong measures such as amalgamation of the unprofitable railways. Interestingly, Simpkin's negotiations in Montreal coincided with an editorial in the *Montreal Star* entitled "Could We Import Mussolini?"

To put the *Montreal Star's* editorial stand in perspective, it must be borne in mind that, at mid-decade, Mussolini was vastly admired by many of the intelligentsia and the well-to-do in Canada. Through state control and public works he had managed to maintain a fairly stable economy. Moreover, in theory the corporate state created a harmonious orchestration of class interests, a much-to-be desired state of affairs in the class-torn Canada of the period. Because fascism had eliminated strikes and other "inefficiencies," a part of the business world in Canada and the United States regarded it favourably. Indeed, *Fortune* magazine devoted an entire issue in 1934 to a favourable analysis of the corporate state and present-day Italy. The Italian dictator was widely regarded as an economic statesman, and his abolition of parliamentary democracy and civil rights was, if anything, approved by his Canadian admirers.

The *Toronto Star*'s foreign correspondent, Pierre Van Passen, had pointed to anti-democratic tendencies in Canada several years earlier: "What has happened in Germany appears of paramount importance to ourselves, for the reason that we seem unconsciously turning up the same or a similar road." He noted the growing demand for state control and above all the clamour for "national governments , concentration cabinets, dictatorial powers." Parliaments, political parties, an independent press were regarded as obstructions to the state in her new tasks. Van Passen saw the possibility of one political group being strengthened at the expense of all others. If that happened, he warned, democracy would give way to fascism. He strongly criticized those who said that society had risen above party government, and reminded them that, under fascism, one political party ran the state, buttressed by the ruthless employment of force. [16]

The kind of thinking deprecated by Van Passen reached its peak early in 1935 when confidence in democratic government and the party system was probably at its lowest ebb. The CUF, therefore, received a hearing from some eminent people. Judges and university professors, as well as big business and the press, were attracted by its Mussolinian ideas, despite the fact they were so inadequately presented by Simpkin. One such supporter was S.A. Jones, an elderly magistrate from Brantford, Ontario. A former president of the Ontario Magistrates' Association, Jones was highly respected for his "good law and good sense." In fact, he was a champion of free speech, having publicly criticized the Toronto police for their repression of soap-box orators. An outspoken partisan of fascism, he wrote a book entitled *Is Fascism the Answer?* and delivered a glowing address on the subject to Toronto's Empire Club in 1934.[17] As a staunch imperialist, he was also impressed with the Mosley trade doctrine based on a self-contained empire. When the CUF came into Ontario, Jones became involved with it. He was in touch with W.F. Elsey, the secretary of the Woodstock branch, and with other sympathizers, including a history professor from the University of Western Ontario, who likewise took to the lecture circuit in praise of fascism.[18]

Others for whom the CUF had a special appeal were the Italian Canadians. The Mosleyites' extravagant admiration for Mussolini created a bond with the Italian community, as did their blackshirt uniform. In Toronto a number of young Italians were active in the CUF, for example, the leader of its youth group was an Italian and so was the editor of its publication, *Fascist Youth* . The CUF catered to the Italian community's natural affection for its homeland by talking up such projects as a Canadian-Italian Bureau to improve relations between the two countries.[19]

During the Ethiopian campaign in 1935–36, nationalism among the Italians in Canada was intensified. Priests joined with the consuls in persuading women to donate their gold wedding rings for the cause and the churches were frequently the scene of Blackshirt ceremonials and emotional appeals for the homeland.[20] Anti-fascist Italians, mostly from socialist-labour circles, had a hard time of it. Pressure to support Mussolini's war effort was so strong that a delegation of anti-fascist Italians from Montreal went to J.S. Woodsworth to complain of intimidation of naturalized Canadians by the consular staff.[21] But these were the exceptions. Most of the hundred thousand Italian Canadians supported the Italian leader and resented the unfriendly press that Mussolini received in English Canada. Typical of their sense of grievance was a letter to the *Globe and Mail* in September 1935 from the president of the Italian War Veterans' Association, complaining of "the unexplainable one-sidedness of a certain type of press." The CUF made a point of sympathizing with the Italian community and nearly two years later was still bemoaning press attacks on Italy during the Ethiopian war, as for instance in W.F. Elsey's article, "The Menace of International Propaganda" which appeared in *The Thunderbolt* in July 1937.

Canadian fascist groups all vied with each other for the support of the Italians. In Montreal Arcand employed an Italian reporter to keep in close touch with the Italian community,[22] and in Winnipeg Whittaker retained an Italian lawyer for the Canadian Nationalist Party.[23] With some encouragement from their parish priests, a number of Italians joined Canadian fascist movements as well as their own. For example, in Windsor the local leader of the Fascisti organized a branch of the Blueshirts.* The tie-in with the Italian-Canadian fascists did not benefit the Canadian fascist groups financially. None of Mussolini's largesse rubbed off on them, since the Italian government confined its subsidies to Canadians of Italian extraction.

When Mussolini invaded Ethiopia he lost his respectability with English-speaking Canadians. No more was said in the press or on the podium about his efficiency, and the close identification of the Canadian Mosleyites with Mussolini's brand of fascism may have had something to do with the fact that their movement never really got started. The effect on fascism in Canada, however, was far less severe than in England. The Ethiopian war ruined Mosley. British public opinion was strongly indignant at the predatory behaviour of Italy and the craven attitude of her own leaders; Canada was less so. Although English-Canadian sympathies were with the Ethiopians, isolationism was so strong that it precluded any real anti-fascist upsurge. French Canada, moreover, continued to be pro-Mussolini and Quebec newspapers of all political stripes were opposed to sanctions against Italy.

---

*Interview with A. Bartelotti, Toronto, January 28, 1974. Mr. Bartelotti was an anarchist in the interwar period and played an active part in the anti-fascist movement.

Duplessis's Quebec

As the decade of the thirties moved into its second half, fascism in Quebec was on the upsurge, carried by a wave of nationalism, anti-semitism and anti-communism. The new international Popular Front of communists and socialists aroused fresh fears and suspicions, and these the fascists played upon. On March 16, 1936, the *Montreal Gazette* reported on a meeting at Maisonneuve market-hall where Salluste Lavery, the fascist mayoralty candidate of 1934, addressed a huge crowd on the evils of the Popular Front, charging that Russia and the Jews were behind it. Speaker after speaker followed him (including a former Conservative MLA) with various denunciations of the Jews, not least of which was a statement that "Hitler is ejecting Jews from Germany. That's what we need here." None of the speakers would answer a question from the floor as to who was sponsoring the meeting, but sitting on the platform was Joseph Ménard, the publisher of *Le Patriote*, and the hall was decorated with blown-up cartoons from that fascist paper.

As for the chief of the fascists, Adrien Arcand, he had now found new and powerful political patrons. The Taschereau administration was ripe to be overthrown and a merger of dissident Liberals under Paul Gouin and the provincial Conservatives, led by Maurice Duplessis, had given birth to a new party, the Union Nationale. Arcand always claimed to be one of its founders,[1] and certainly he was its first publicist; in February 1936 he began editing a daily tabloid, *L'Illustration Nouvelle*, which functioned as a semi-official organ for the Union Nationale party. While Arcand might have been expected to have more in common with Gouin, whose ideas on corporatism he praised in *Le Patriote,* it was the traditional Conservative, Maurice Duplessis, with whom he allied. When Duplessis became premier in the summer of 1936, Arcand's influence expanded accordingly.

The Duplessis government provided a salubrious climate for Arcand and his friends. Not only did he become the editor of the semi-official *L'Illustration Nouvelle,* but his old associate, Joseph Ménard, was equally the recipient of government favour. In September 1936 *Le Patriote* closed down. Ménard was immediately hired by Duplessis's Minister of Colonization, H.L. Auger. According to the editor of *L'Autorité,* Auger "had never hidden his sympathy for *Le Patriote.*" Certainly as a Montreal alderman, before becoming a provincial cabinet minister, he had distinguished himself by an unrelenting anti-semitism. For example, in the autumn of 1933 he sparked considerable controversy at City Hall with a resolution calling for a total ban on Jewish immigration. For this stand he was praised in the pages of *Le Patriote* and *L'Action Nationale.* In the summer of 1937 it was rumoured that Ménard (who had just left the Ministry of Colonization) was going to "resuscitate" *Le Patriote,* and that the paper would be "principally supported by ministerial announcements and printing contracts."[2] Ménard's father had recently died and, presumably with his inheritance, he had managed to buy a printing shop and was already producing a government publication, *Le Colon (The Colonist).* The rumour about *Le Patriote* also proved correct; on October 21, 1937, Ménard resumed publication of his slander sheet.

While Ménard was free to pursue his habitual attacks on the Jews, Arcand, as befitted the editor of a respectable paper, had to eschew overt anti-semitism. In fact, Arcand's tenure was contingent on his good behaviour in this regard. The behind-the-scenes owner of *L'Illustration Nouvelle* was Eugène Berthiaume of the *La Presse* publishing family, who lived in Paris where he acted as Canadian consul.[3] Berthiaume gave Arcand a generally free hand, but he was said to have placed a man on staff to see that Arcand kept anti-semitism out of the paper.[4]

The main theme of Duplessis and *L'Illustration Nouvelle* was the alleged threat of communism in French Canada. For Duplessis it was a camouflage for his alliance with Anglo-Saxon big business, "the trusts," which he had promised to curb in his election campaign. For Arcand it was an old weapon to be used against the Jews who were identified in the public mind with the communists. Actually communism was almost non-existent in Quebec. The Depression turned French Canadians into more extreme nationalists rather than into communists or socialists. Only in the industrial areas of Montreal did the Communist Party have any following and even there it regularly polled only a few thousand votes.[5] In January 1938 an Anglo-Canadian journalist estimated that there were twenty fascists for every communist in Quebec.[6] Anti-communism was as safe a platform as motherhood, both of which were strongly promoted by the Catholic church.

Pius XI had condemned communism as the destroyer of the family and of society, and the ultramontane clergy of Quebec, led by Cardinal Villeneuve, outdid the pope in their zeal. Even French-Canadian nationalists admitted that the church was more zealous in condemning communism than fascism.[7] In the first place, the Catholic clergy ardently admired Mussolini. Moreover, the fascist doctrine of corporatism was popular with the clergy. Sanctioned by papal encyclical, it was lauded by Cardinal Villeneuve and the hierarchy as the finest expression of social justice. Thus the French Canadians, a church-going people, heard a great deal about the dangers of communism and very little about those of fascism.

The Spanish Civil War, which began in the summer of 1936, intensified French-Canadian anti-communism. The Quebec clergy was violently opposed to the Spanish Republican government side because of its Soviet backing and its anti-clericalism. Charges of Republican atrocities upon the Spanish clergy (reproduced in full in *Le Devoir* and *L'Action Nationale*) understandably whipped up Quebec public opinion against communism. When a visiting delegation of Spanish Republicans was scheduled to speak at a public meeting in Montreal in October 1936, there was such a violent student protest that the mayor cancelled the permit for the meeting. In the aftermath, the vociferous students were publicly praised by Premier Duplessis for hindering "communists" from speaking. Eugene Forsey, then a young lecturer at McGill, was so outraged by this denial of the sponsoring group's civil liberties, as well as by the gratuitous insult to Spain's legal government, that he wrote to the federal Minister of Justice, Ernest Lapointe:

This affair was carefully organized; former students of mine have in their possession one of the notes sent round ordering the youths to meet at the headquarters of the Jeunesse Ouvrière Catholique and "bring their canes". It is obvious also that it has approval in high quarters. There is, in fact, a formidable Fascist movement in this province.[8]

He proceeded to compare what was happening in Quebec with the beginnings of fascism in Italy and with what he himself had witnessed in Berlin in the summer of 1932.

As this affair indicates, it was the youth to whom fascism appealed. They formed an important sector of the rank and file in Arcand's party. As in other places, the young people of Quebec were carried away by the apparent dynamism of the movement under the leadership of the intense Arcand, who modelled his style upon the continental dictators. The appeal to youth was unanimously attested to; the Liberal politicians, Adelard Godbout and T.D. Bouchard, and the outspoken, anti-fascist journalist, J.D. Harvey, all stressed the point.[9] Similarly, a Liberal MLA told the Quebec legislature that young men were being enrolled by the hundreds weekly in the fascist movement. In the Lapointe Papers there is a sorrowing letter from a Montreal man telling the Minister of Justice that his sons had been converted by Arcand.[10]

Nevertheless, the zeal of his youthful followers caused Arcand serious problems. Strong nationalists and Catholics, they were suspicious of his leanings towards imperialism and disturbed by his obvious preference for the irreligious Nazis over the Italian fascists whom they themselves admired. Without question there was a division in the party. In his aspiration to lead a national movement, Arcand had adopted the imperialist position of the Anglo-Canadian fascist groups in western Canada. Moreover, he had by this time fallen under the influence of Mosley, who was a staunch proponent of empire. The issue came to a head when the National Social Christian Party's program was published and it specifically called for "more active participation in the interests of the British Empire on the basis of an equal partnership." According to a rather facetious report in *Le Devoir,* this led to a passing revolt against the "Pontifex Maximus." It seemed that the young Quebec nationalists were demanding reassurance from Arcand on the Catholic and French-Canadian nature of the party. Furthermore, they were insisting that three of their number be appointed to the Grand Council, whose secret members were known to be predominantly middle-aged. At first the high-handed Arcand refused to be called to account, but since the dissidents were in the majority, the next issue of *Le Fasciste Canadien* in February 1937 promised that party policy would not sanction participation in a war unless first approved by plebiscite. Apparently the other less basic issues were cleared up because the threatened schism was averted.

In the winter of 1937 the National Social Christian Party had seven hundred card-carrying members. This came out when some of the dissidents managed to get a look at the membership lists. They discovered that the vaunted strength of two thousand members was accounted for by the simple subterfuge of starting the numbers at a thousand. Despite their relatively small numbers, *Le Devoir* considered that the fascists were a zealous corps[11], and the range of their sympathizers can only be conjectured.

As fascist aggression abroad and rumours of war became the stuff of daily news, Arcand's little party began to look more ominous. Its emblem—a swastika wreathed in maple leaves and surmounted by a beaver—graphically suggested that Nazism could become Canadianized. *Le Fasciste Canadien* had graduated from a mimeographed sheet and was now a magazine printed on the same presses as the semi-governmental tabloid, *L'Illustration Nouvelle*. The fascists appeared to be well organized, with all of Montreal divided into zones, and other zones in the province at large, notably a strong one of approximately a hundred members at St. Hyacinthe. Hundreds of people turned out for the mass rallies at the Monument National when Arcand, sporting a Hitler moustache, screamed in approved dictator style. (The audiences were not always as obedient as those in Germany. There was often heckling that had to be silenced by the blue-shirted "storm troopers.")

Indeed, the party was taking on a paramilitary character. Youths and veterans, wearing the regulation blue shirt, were marching and drilling under the baton of a martinet named Major Joseph Maurice Scott. Scott came from an old French and Scottish family of St. Hyacinthe. An outstanding athlete, he had been on two Canadian Olympic teams and had taught physical training at the Royal Military College in Kingston, Ontario. During the war he had been a recruiting officer and physical training instructor with the Canadian Expeditionary Force . A bull of a man, with a thick neck and shaven head, Scott had dragooned many a French Canadian into the army. During prohibition, as chief of the Quebec Liquor Commission's private police, he had found congenial work looking for smugglers. When Duplessis was elected Scott lost his job in a purge of the police; he was now a fuel merchant, selling insurance on the side, and reported to be very bitter about his dismissal.[12] His association with Arcand did not recover his job for him, but training fascist "legions" was exactly his kind of work. Besides, he idolized Arcand. Speaking at a rally in St. Hyacinthe in December 1937, he told a home-town audience that "soon Fascists will be everywhere, from Gaspé to Abitibi. You will have them in your doors, at your windows, beside you."[13]

In imitation of Mussolini's corporate state, the National Social Christian Party had a Grand Council composed of Arcand's lieutenants. Ménard had faded into the background. Chief among the new supporters at this time were Dr. Gabriel Lambert and J.E. Lessard. The latter was a policeman by training who had been a provincial detective and before that a member of the RCMP in the West. [14] He was in charge of the officer corps of the Blueshirts. A newspaper photograph in *Le Fasciste Canadien* (December 1937) shows about a hundred and fifty of these fascist officers at a dinner in a St. Catherine Street cafe: it is jarringly reminiscent of pictures taken at the Brown House in Munich just before Hitler came to power.

Dr. Lambert was reputed by some to be a rich man, by others only moderately successful. In any event, he was a disappointed man because he had been unable to promote his pet theory that the eye was the body's mirror and that diagnoses could be made by studying the retina. Having failed to start a cult, it is perhaps not surprising that Lambert turned to other schemes; and Arcand's movement was a natural for him since he was intensely anti-semitic. Described as "a stoutish, sweet-talking, suave professional man, affecting a pince nez," his senatorial presence lent dignity to the shabby proceedings of the fascists, and Arcand took him everywhere with him.[15]

As well read in the literature of anti-semitism as Arcand himself, Lambert made a major contribution to it with a pamphlet entitled "The Key to the Mystery." A compilation of excerpts from all the standard texts on the subject (including many taken out of context from Jewish writers), it was undoubtedly the most vicious defamation of the Jewish people ever published in Canada. Thousands of copies were turned out, printed in both French and English. The Canadian Jewish Congress became alarmed by its mass distribution, and a correspondence of sorts ensued between the executive secretary and Lambert. In letters addressed to "Jew Caiserman, Talmudist," Lambert denied editing the pamphlet, but for that matter he also denied the established fact that he was an official of the National Social Christian Party.[16] The Congress was also disturbed because it had it on good authority that this hate propaganda was printed on the presses of *L'Illustration Nouvelle*.[17]

In fact a deluge of hate literature was emanating from Arcand's headquarters, some of it produced locally but most originating from Germany. A letter to Arcand from Germany dated March 31, 1937 reads in part, "I am enclosing tracts of the latest issue of Fichte-Bund . . . ." Arcand denied that he distributed German material but his party's rubber stamp mark was on hundreds of such pamphlets. Much of *Le Fasciste Canadien* was simply translations of German articles, and the speeches of Hitler, Goering and Goebbels received front-page coverage. Arcand himself contributed anti-semitic articles tailored for the home market such as "We Won't Fight for the Rothschilds," "1837 and the Jews," and "Our French Comrades Menaced by Jewish Communists."

There were other local propagandists, none, however, as prolific as Arcand. One was his early backer, Dr. P.E. Lalanne, who was reputed to be treasurer of the National Social Christian Party.[18] Lalanne's pamphlet "Why We Should Oppose the Jew" was first presented as a lecture in Ottawa, under the auspices of the Native Sons of Canada;[19] like Salluste Lavery, Arcand's lawyer and supporter, Lalanne was an active member of that organization. Another propaganda-writer was Jean Tissot, the Ottawa policeman convicted of libel against A.J. Freiman. After his dismissal from the Ottawa police department for his fascist activities, Tissot was hired as chief of police in Rouyn, Quebec. It was no coincidence that Rouyn became the northern distribution centre for fascist literature.[20]

Some of the hate propaganda fell on fertile ground. Parish

priests used it to update the age-old religious prejudices against the Jews. In September 1937 a parish paper pronounced:

> All countries are unanimous in recognizing that we have no greater enemy than the Jews. They are the source of all great cataclysms. They participated in the French Revolution and the Russian Revolution. They are the most fervent leaders of Freemasonry, the promoters of discord, the agitators of strikes, and finally they are the propagandists of Communism.[21]

Another instance occurred at a Social Credit meeting in a Montreal church hall where a priest ranted violently against the Jews. A member of the audience was so concerned that he wrote to Cardinal Villeneuve about it: "You are undoubtedly aware that an intense anti-Jewish campaign is being pursued in all parts of the province of Quebec and most especially in the metropolis of Montreal."[22] But the cardinal, in classic bureaucratic fashion, merely referred him to the Archbishop of Montreal. The *Fédération des Clubs Ouvriers* also continued its unremitting opposition to equality for Jewish citizens. On learning that a Jewish alderman had been selected by his colleagues to act as deputy mayor, the Maisonneuve branch sent a letter of protest to City Hall.[23]

The influential *Le Devoir* contributed to the unfortunate situation. Although no friend to Arcand, the paper had become intensely anti-semitic under the direction of Georges Pelletier. On April 17, 1937, Pelletier published an editorial on "Anti-Semitism, Growing Peril." In it he quoted extensively from a Dutch author who appears to have compiled a book not unlike Lambert's "Key to the Mystery." At pains to show his own objectivity and that of his sources, Pelletier described the book in question as "moderate in tone, laden with authentic quotations from Talmud and Jewish authors." It is, in fact, stock hate literature, proferring the familiar arguments of the Protocols:

> What above all worries non-Jews is the feeling of harbouring portions of another people, who are unassimilable, from a nation which aims at the domination of the world and of whom several members foment revolutions . . . .

On this premise, the author declares (and Pelletier agrees) that the only solution is to expel all Jews from their present countries and send them to Palestine. Even long-assimilated English and French Jews must accept this forced "Zionism." Any who manage to evade deportation are to be divested of all rights of citizenship. As Pelletier paraphrased the Dutch author,

> The voluntary repatriation of some, the forced incorporation of others, the establishment of an imposed Jewish passport, will make all those who would like to live in other countries aliens, where they will no longer have any rights other than those granted to aliens.

Neither the intellectual anti-semitism of *Le Devoir* nor the racial prejudice of parish priests and worker organizations was mitigated by official statements of good will towards the Jewish community, as in the time of Taschereau. Instead, Duplessis showed himself tolerant in the extreme even towards Arcand's movement.

Meanwhile, in 1937 the provincial government had brought in the so-called Padlock Act, enabling the Attorney General (Duplessis himself) to padlock premises allegedly used for the propagation of communism. The legislation was Duplessis's answer to Mackenzie King's repeal of section 98 of the Criminal Code. It is indicative of the anti-communist sentiment in Quebec that the bill passed unanimously, sailing through the Legislative Assembly with three readings in half an hour. Within a few months, the office of the communist paper, *La Clarté,* and its editor's house were padlocked, as well as a printing company and a leftist book store. Private homes were also raided, almost, it seemed, at random. One woman listed the spoils taken by the police after ransacking her library: a biography of Woodsworth, a book on Spinoza, some social research pamphlets, and a popular news magazine with a picture of Trotsky on the cover.[24]

Liberal reaction to the Padlock Act was swift, with the formation of a Civil Liberties Union. The moving spirit was R.L. Calder, long a watch-dog of civil rights in Quebec. Hoping to force the federal government to disallow the act, Calder began stumping the country, calling it "the rottenest piece of legislation ever drawn up" and telling his audiences that it had resulted from a conference of Duplessis officials with Cardinal Villeneuve. Despite the outrage of

Anglo-Canadian liberals, the Padlock Act was not disallowed. King and Lapointe knew it had the full support of the people, the parties, and the priests in Quebec province.

The irony was that fascist propaganda could still be freely distributed in Quebec. Not only anti-semitism, but all the themes of international fascism were being propagated by Arcand. In December 1937 the Quebec paper *Le Jour* made a list of them: scorn of the Canadian constitution, a campaign against the vote and against the institution of parliament, exaltation of race, incitement of ferocious hatred among nationalities, exploitation of anti-capitalism, a fight against liberty of speech, suppression of unions, and appeal to violence and mutiny. All this material was distributed anonymously through the simple expedient of renting a post office box.

In an effort to stop the use of post office box numbers for this purpose, the Canadian Jewish Congress made representation to the Postmaster General, who appointed a special investigator to look into the matter. On opening Arcand's box himself, the officer discovered a batch of literature from Germany, but he confided to one of the Jewish members of parliament that "with the exception of one employee, there was no one in the entire post office organization in Montreal whom he could appoint to watch the box."[25] This charge that the Montreal post office was a receptacle of fascists was made more than once. The same was alleged of the Customs department in that city where employees were said to give the fascist salute openly and to pass around propaganda.*

In August 1937, H.M. Caiserman sent a brief to the prime minister on behalf of the Canadian Jewish Congress, protesting the circulation of hate literature. He requested that post office boxes no longer be available for this use and furthermore that legal means be adopted to make such libels a criminal offence. Alternatively, the brief suggested the setting up of a royal commission to study the whole question of fascist activity in Canada. Caiserman enclosed some samples of Arcand's material, including "The Key to the Mystery," which sufficiently shocked one of Mackenzie King's

---

*P.A.C., Lapointe Papers, vol. 22, Thomas Vien, M.P. to Lapointe, July 18, 1939. This allegation was made by a constituent of the Montreal M.P., and the latter passed it on to the Minister of Justice.

bland secretaries into describing them as "strongly anti-semitic in nature and, in some cases, of a very obnoxious character."[26] Nevertheless, the prime minister's staff was planning to spare him this unpleasantness until A.J. Freiman, a personal friend of King's and his summer neighbour at Kingsmere, called to ask him to look at the file personally. A memorandum shows that the Cabinet did consider the question of anti-semitic activities in Canada as a result of the Caiserman brief; but nothing was done beyond referring the matter back to the Postmaster General and to the Department of Justice.[27]

The Jewish Congress brief also informed the government that Arcand's group had met in secret session with fascists in Toronto on August 21, and that "their decisions as reported to us aim at our annihilation." This was reliable information. Arcand had indeed made his first tentative move into Ontario and had laid plans for an Ontario division of the National Social Christian Party. Even a leader had been chosen, a young Toronto fascist named John Ross Taylor.[28]

Arcand's group was also flexing its muscles publicly. When Tim Buck, the leader of the Communist Party of Canada, and a communist deputy from France were scheduled to speak at the Montreal Arena in October 1937, the fascists openly stage-managed a student protest. Prominent among the otherwise young protesters assembled on the steps of City Hall was the portly Dr. Lambert. Lambert, in fact, acted as a spokesman, and among other incendiary statements, shouted out that two thousand fascists were ready to aid the students if necessary.[29] Mayor Raynault quickly agreed to ban the communist meeting "as it might lead to disorder," later admitting candidly that he had been glad of the pretext of the student riot to do so.[30] (It is worth recalling that in 1932 Raynault had protested against the Bercovitch bill as prejudicial to freedom of speech.) The fascist influence on the students was further demonstrated that evening when, not to be done out of their riot by the mayor's ready compliance, they roamed around the vicinity of the Arena, carrying canes and (to quote the *Montreal Gazette*) "raised their strong right arms in the fascist salute." There was some smashing of Jewish shop windows before the night was over.

The Civil Liberties Union leapt in to protest this latest abrogation of free speech. R.L. Calder applied for a warrant for the arrest of Lambert and one of the student leaders, on the charge of inciting to riot. However, the judge refused to grant any warrants, expressing the opinion that the students might have gone to prevent rather than cause a breach of the peace. An outraged Calder stormed out of the court.[31]

The issue generated more heat when Cardinal Villeneuve gave public approval to the student demonstration and Mayor Raynault's stand. "Under pretext of respecting a morbid democracy," he thundered, "people wave at us the spectre of an illusory fascism, and meanwhile the enemies gain a foothold and make a mockery of our judicial scruples."[32] Strong words, and very revealing of the prelate's papally-inspired anti-democratic views. At this, Calder made his next move. Obtaining an order from the Chief Justice, he had Lambert summoned before a police court on a charge of inciting to riot.

The fascists milked as much publicity as possible from the Lambert trial. They came to court in their blue shirts; they gave the fascist salute; Lambert declared under oath that he was a fascist; and outside the court house, student supporters passed out anti-semitic pamphlets. At one session Arcand put in an appearance, in civilian clothes but flanked by a twenty-man guard of Blueshirts. He and his followers were understandably cocky. With the premier and the cardinal supporting the riot, the fascists had every reason to be confident. It is revealing of public opinion, however, that the reaction of the spectators to the Blueshirts was one of amusement. Perhaps the sight of the stout, bald, middle-aged Lambert, with his pince-nez, dressed up as a *gauleiter* was just too much for Canadian common sense. It appeared that the only danger to the self-styled Nazis was being laughed out of court. [33]

The case proceeded to criminal court where the same judge who had refused the warrants was presiding. Calder immediately moved for an adjournment, claiming that the judge was "already decided by temperament in favour of the fascist accused." Red in the face with anger, His Honour adjourned the case. But when it resumed two months later, the same judge was again on the bench. Not too surprisingly, the charge against Lambert was dismissed.

Although the dogged Calder immediately started further legal action, the Lambert case was a great triumph for Arcand's movement. Lambert's picture appeared in out-of-town as well as local

1. *A* Goglu *cartoon attacking the*
    Bercovitch Bill (20th January
    1933).

2. *"We must not buy meat from Jewish butchers".* Le Patriote's achat Chez Nous *Campaign, 13th of June, 1935.*

3. *Adrien Arcand*

4.   Dr. Gabriel Lambert

5.   Major Joseph Maurice Scott

6.   Joseph Farr

7. Major Scott (centre),
   Commander-in-Chief of Arcand's
   legions, in council with his
   officers.

8. Dr. Lambert with Adrien
   Arcand, giving the Fascist salute
   to the judge at his 1937 trial for
   inciting to riot.

9. *Major Scott gives the Fascist salute in front of the insignia of the National Social Christian Party.*

10. *Fascist Legionnaires drilling in Montreal in January, 1938.*

11. *A meeting of the National Social Christian Party early in 1938. In the foreground (left to right) Mme Arcand, Arcand, and Joseph Farr.*

12. *The eleven Fascist leaders of the National Unity Party at the preliminary enquiry in June, 1940, which led to their internment. Farr and Scott are on the extreme left and Arcand is in the centre.*

13. *"After the Demonstration" from*
The Thunderbolt, *June 1938.*

papers. Even the "national" *Globe and Mail* put him on its front page. Embittered by his experiences, Calder did not mince words. "Fascism in Quebec," he told his audiences in the other provinces, "is encouraged by bench, pulpit and council chamber."[34]

At the same time, Arcand was moving up in international fascist circles. In 1936 he met Henry H. Beamish, a kind of roving ambassador for world fascism, when the latter was passing through Canada. Beamish was very impressed with him and Arcand became a protégé of his. Indeed Beamish said of him:

> After Adolf Hitler, I consider Adrien Arcand the one leader who stands out far above any others I have met, as he has all the necessary flair, vim and originality which a real leader requires. A Catholic of course, as are all French Canadians, but he knows exactly how far he can use and trust the clerical element. At the first sign of a Jew-Bolshevist upheaval in Canada, he is in a position to take over the government of the country.[35]

It was likely on Beamish's recommendation that Arcand was invited to speak, along with Beamish himself and other fascist leaders, at a mammoth rally staged by the German-American Bund in the New York Hippodrome on October 31, 1937. On the platform with Fritz Kuhn was the Bundist Rudolph Markman, John Fumizio from the Italo-American fascists, and William Pelley, leader of the American fascists, the Silvershirts. These men flattered Arcand; he was wined and dined at the Harvard Club, and there was a good deal of talk about linking up the American and Canadian organizations.

Arcand returned to Canada in a euphoric state of mind. *Le Fasciste Canadien* for December 1937 announced to the faithful that the rally in New York marked the official beginning of fascism in America. Losing all sense of reality, Arcand claimed to have eighty thousand followers in Montreal alone. He boasted that if an election were held at that time, his party would win twenty seats; by spring they would double that figure. He declared 1938 the year of the National Social Christian Party, and predicted it would spread across the country. These visionary statements were widely quoted and rocketed Arcand into the national news.

Confronted with the increasing national notoriety of a fascist movement within its province, the Duplessis government preserved a discreet silence. The provincial Liberals, however, denounced Arcand and his works in the strongest terms. "What is Monsieur Duplessis Waiting For?" the Liberal leader, T.D. Bouchard, enquired editorially in his St. Hyacinthe paper *En Avant* in November. People should stop smiling at the antics of the fascists, he warned, because they were a real threat to freedom and democracy. Adelard Godbout flatly told a Quebec City audience that the dangerous menace in the province was not communism—the people would never be taken in by that—it was fascism. And J.C. Harvey, the editor of *Le Jour*, demanded that the fascist "gangsters" be stopped. He knew the leaders, he told his readers. "Some are degenerates. Others are corrupt or stupidly sectarian. All are dangerous because they cultivate dishonest means to attain their ends: lies, hypocrisy, calumny, blackmail, intimidation and gulling." No wonder Arcand threatened to stand Harvey against a wall when he became dictator!

Arcand Moves into Canada

When Arcand slipped into Toronto in the summer of 1937, Ontario gave signs of being ready for him. Anti-semitism there had become more open, more institutionalized, and more respectable than a few years earlier. Incidents of discrimination, played up by the press, undoubtedly encouraged the attempted fascist penetration into the heart of English-speaking Canada.

The first reported incidents occurred at private tennis and golf clubs. The exclusion of Jews from most of these was nothing new; it was precisely because they could not get into the established clubs that they had formed their own. But social anti-semitism assumed a new dimension when the Jewish tennis club made application to the Toronto Tennis League and was refused. Apparently a few clubs in the league had given notice that they would withdraw if the Jewish club was admitted, and the others agreed to turn down the application. According to the *Globe and Mail*,

> The executive of the Jewish club accepted the situation philo-sophically and unanimously voted to frown upon any attempts to capitalize on the discrimination against them, even agreeing to explain the situation to the members by word of mouth and urge them to avoid precipitating any crisis in the League.[1]

It is only too understandable why Jews in the 1930s were anxious to avoid confrontations. Horrified at events in Germany, they were afraid of stirring up a backlash that could endanger their own security. Living through the nightmare of the Nazi era, they may have been subconsciously haunted by a fear of violence. At any rate, they were ready to overlook social discrimination, even that verging on ostracism as in the case of the Tennis League.

St. Andrew's golf club, one of the few Toronto clubs with some Jewish members, was the scene of the next incident. A large sign suddenly appeared at the entrance reading : "After Sunday, June 20, this course will be restricted to Gentiles only. Please do not question this policy." It was signed by the club secretary. The ban applied to green fee players, as well as to members and guests. When approached by the press, the secretary explained that the new ruling was due to pressure from Gentile members. "We had to protect our business," he said. "The great majority of our people are Gentiles and we had to respect their wishes." The anti-semitic policy took the Jewish members by surprise. Why out of a clear blue sky this sort of thing should happen mystified them.

A more familiar type of Toronto anti-semitism flared up at the East End Beaches a few weeks later. Scrawled across a breakwater, in letters three feet high, appeared the words: "Britain gave you Jerusalem—for God's sake leave us this beach." Although inaccurate—the 1937 partition plan for Palestine placed Jerusalem in British hands—the message was perfectly clear. In reporting the incident, the *Globe and Mail* probably contributed inadvertently to the Hitlerian image of the Jew as pariah, by commenting that although very few Jews swam at this particular stretch of beach, "some residents believed that the sign was painted by individuals who feared the newly found place might be used by Jewish people."[2]

Anonymous hate messages and discriminatory policies at private recreation clubs were far removed from the official character of Nazi anti-semitism. But from the town of Galt in southern Ontario came echoes of Hitlerism when the mayor publicly called an alderman "a bloody Jew" and declared, "I have no more respect for a Jew than Hitler has. It is time he was told he was a Hebrew, and what a Gentile thinks of a Hebrew."[3] Such remarks from an elected representative of the people indicate the deterioration in the status of Ontario Jews.

This worsening of Christian-Jewish relations must be charged to the contagion of Nazi propaganda. Hitler had done his work only too well, and by his example had released the inhibitions of latent anti-semites everywhere. The Nuremburg Decrees of 1935 had deprived German Jews of their basic citizenship rights and outlawed them from the fabric of German society; moreover, thousands were known to be in concentration camps for no other reason than their Jewishness. Banished to a netherworld by the august authority of a duly constituted government, Jews appeared to be a legitimate target for abuse—more particularly, since Britain was assiduously cultivating the friendship of Hitler.

In May 1937 Neville Chamberlain replaced Stanley Baldwin as prime minister, and appeasement of the dictators became the official British policy. It had no stronger booster than Mackenzie King. In London for the Imperial Conference that spring, he resolved to make a "strenuous effort to understand Nazi Germany," and before sailing home, visited Berlin. According to newspaper reports, he had a long talk with Hitler, which he found "most interesting and most valuable," and spent an enjoyable evening at the opera with Goering. On his return, he assured the Canadian people that Germany did not want war any more than England did.[4] Perhaps King was predisposed to find Hitler amiable, since his government had just signed a trade agreement with Nazi Germany.

There was little objection to doing business with Hitler. In the House of Commons, the Jewish M.P. from Toronto, Sam Factor, was a voice in the wilderness in opposing his party's German trade policy, while only the leftists criticized King for his "friendly overtures" to Hitler.[5] Most English as well as French Canadians were totally behind appeasement. Generally speaking, there was indifference to Nazism, which was regarded as just another nationalist movement, and it was widely believed that Hitler would be satisfied when he recovered the lands lost by the Treaty of Versailles. While Mussolini had alienated English Canada with his invasion of Ethiopia, Hitler was considered justified in taking back the Rhineland.[6] As for the Nazi treatment of the Jewish minority, that was strictly an internal matter. A majority of Canadians would have disagreed with the League of Nations Commissioner for German Refugees, James G. McDonald, when he stated that "when domestic policies threaten the demoralization and exile of hundreds of thousands of human beings, considerations of diplomatic correctness must yield to those of common humanity." [7] As the Canadian political scientist, James Eayrs, has pointed out, Canada got its news of Germany from the whitewash reports of the British ambassador in Berlin and from its own High Commissioner in London, Vincent Massey, whose views were coloured by his association with the Cliveden Set—a group of influential appeasers who frequented the country house of Lord and Lady Astor.[8] Compounding these reassuring interpretations of Nazi Germany was Mackenzie King's false assessment of Hitler in 1937.*

A newspaper poll of Toronto theatre managers in the autumn of 1937 affords some insight into the Canadian perception of Hitler. Asked to describe audience response to various public figures appearing in the newsreels they reported that moviegoers laughed at Mussolini and booed the Japanese but showed no reaction to Hitler.[9] The strutting, screaming, diabolical figure on the screen was not yet regarded as a monster by the average Canadian. Fervently anxious to avoid war, like his prime minister he was prepared to give Hitler the benefit of every doubt.

The complacency about fascism was in sharp contrast to the exaggerated fears about communism. Although Toronto was the headquarters of the Communist Party of Canada and several card-carrying members held municipal office, the total membership in the country was estimated at under fifteen thousand. Yet Torontonians saw communists everywhere. In part this was due to the Oshawa strike in the spring of 1937, an event which evoked some of the same horror as the Winnipeg strike of 1919. While the American-based Congress of Industrial Organizations (CIO) gained a tentative foothold in Ontario as a result, the strike caused public opinion to swing to the right. Premier Mitchell Hepburn dropped his two most progressive cabinet ministers, David Croll and Arthur Roebuck; (in 1935 the latter had attributed an improved attitude to Jews to the presence of progressives like himself in the seats of power.)[10] Forming an undeclared triumvirate with McCullagh of the *Globe* and George Drew (then an aspiring politician of uncertain political stripe), Hepburn incited the province against industrial unionism by branding it as Bolshevism. The *Globe* editorials and Drew's cam-

*On his return from Europe, King told Bruce Hutchison that Hitler was "a simple sort of peasant," not very intelligent and no serious danger to anyone. B. Hutchison, *The Incredible Canadian* (Toronto, 1953), p.226.

paign speeches went one step further and identified the CIO and communism with Jews. "Although it cannot be said that a majority of Jews are Communists," stated one editorial, "the indications are that a large percentage, and probably a majority of Communists are Jews."[11] (To answer this kind of unsubstantiated charge, the Committee on Gentile-Jewish Relations that same year published "Facts and Fancies About Jews," in which it was estimated that of the fifteen thousand Communist Party members in Canada, only four hundred and fifty were Jewish. This statistic, in turn, was unsubstantiated. In actual fact, however, while there were Jews, notably J.B. Salsberg, who were prominent in the Ontario party leadership, most of its leaders were Clydeside Scots or Englishmen like Tim Buck.) Drew was more subtle. Without actually stating that communists were Jews, he made the point by larding his anti-CIO speeches with Jewish names.[12] A woman reader accused the *Globe and Mail* of fostering fascism and asked columnist McAree, "Don't you think that despite Colonel Drew's talk of British democracy, he stinks of Germany and fascism since his return from Europe?" Agnes MacPhail, a United Farmer M.P. and the only woman in the House of Commons, also warned of the spread of fascism: "I am not one who lies awake at night worrying about Communism in Canada. I think the danger in Canada is fascism.[13]

Miss MacPhail was more of a prophet than she knew. Two weeks later Arcand and Lambert were sitting in a room on Bay Street with John Ross Taylor and other Toronto fascists. The twenty-four-year-old Taylor came from a solid middle-class background; his father was a lawyer and his grandfather had been a prosperous manufacturer and alderman around the turn of the century.* After much discussion it was decided to make young Taylor the leader of an English-speaking wing of Arcand's *Parti National Social Chrétien* to be translated as the National Christian Party of Canada. It was also decided to have him run in a Jewish district in the forthcoming provincial election.

Arcand was now corresponding with Sir Oswald Mosley on a

---

*Brochure re Taylor's candidacy in Toronto civic election 1972. In this election Taylor ran in Ward 11 for the Western Guard. (Toronto Municipal Archives).

very friendly basis;* the scheme hatched in the secret session, to run a candidate in the heavily Jewish riding of St. Andrews, was clearly patterned on Mosley's tactics of "jew-baiting"—a repulsive term of the epoch constantly used by both friends and foes of the Jewish people. In 1936 Mosley had begun a campaign of provoking London's East End Jews by marching through their district and conducting street-corner harangues. When this activity was curtailed by the Public Order Act of the same year, he turned to political action and in March 1937 the British Union of Fascists contested several London County Council elections in the East End. Actually Mosley was a spent force by 1937 but his Canadian admirer did not know it. Arcand adopted his techniques of provocation, as well as his "solution to the Jewish problem"—forced emigration to Madagascar.

Taylor's campaign consisted of blanketing the Jewish district with thousands of election handbills which read like a perverted travel poster: "Jews to Madagascar—one of the garden spots of the world." It displayed his picture and described him openly as a "fascist candidate." But the real message, urging a boycott of Jewish merchants, was on the reverse side. Under the headline "Shall the Unscrupulous Jew Eliminate the Gentile in Canadian Business?" was a drawing of an octopus with tentacles labelled "radio stations . . . realty . . . hotels . . . department stores . . . manufacturing . . . banking"[14]—the "Jewish octopus" was a well-worn item of anti-semitic propaganda. Taylor and his helpers also flooded the district with pamphlets from Germany. While denying any affiliation with the Nazis, Taylor invited such assumptions by wearing a swastika on his lapel and giving the Nazi salute. The alliance with Arcand was hinted at in his boast that he would be protected by a bodyguard of Blueshirts, the uniform of Arcand's followers.

The labour movement and the liberal clergy were the groups that protested most vocally against Toronto's little Nazis. Under pressure from these quarters, the Toronto City Council sought legal advice to see if Taylor could be prosecuted but learned that group

---

*For example, when, in the autumn of 1937, Mosley was hit with a stone in Liverpool and landed in the hospital, Arcand sent a telegram of commiseration: "You proved at your life's peril Britons are no more at home in Britain and aliens rule the streets. More urgent than ever to free nations for their nationals." Cited in *Toronto Star*, June 19, 1940.

libel could not be suppressed through existing procedures. Then J.J. Glass a Jewish Liberal M.P.P. and candidate for re-election in the riding where Taylor was threatening to run, told his Jewish constituents that the Hepburn government was considering introducing legislation to outlaw hate literature.

Glass had been interested for some time in getting group libel legislation in Ontario. Inspired by the successful Tobias case in Winnipeg, in 1935 he had talked of introducing a law similar to the one in Manitoba. The response, however, had not been encouraging. The *Globe* had ridiculed the idea in an editorial entitled "Why Be Touchy?" and a spokesman for the Orangemen declared that group libel legislation would be a curb on free speech and a backward step.

On October 6, 1937, the Hepburn government was re-elected, its scare campaign linking the CIO with the communists having paid off handsomely in the conservative temper of the times. In St. Andrews riding, Glass topped the poll; Taylor had not run after all, owing to dissension in the ranks of his followers. That the dissemination of fascist propaganda had been the primary objective in Taylor's abortive campaign for office anyway was clear from the continuing stream which swamped the city after the election. In the midst of it all, the highly regarded young rabbi of the reform temple, Maurice Eisendrath, found a swastika and funeral crepe nailed to his front door on Hallowe'en. "What happened on my doorstep is of little moment," he told the press, "but what is happening throughout Canada is vitally significant."[15] He charged that Nazi agents based in Toronto, Montreal and Winnipeg were spreading anti-semitic propaganda and he declared that the federal government should take action.

It was at this point that Glass announced his intention of introducing a group libel law into the provincial legislature. The *Globe and Mail* reacted sharply. Such legislation was "not the British way." It would be "mischievous, undemocratic and anti-British." A law to curb so-called anti-semitic activities would give all groups, communists and fascists included, the right to protection. (The editorial writer did not pause to reflect that only falsehoods were potentially libellous.) There would be no limit to what might be construed as "anti" in court actions. Such a law would lead to fascism itself. The writer advised "the Hebrews" to ignore the propaganda and, pouring salt in their wounds, went on to say that "if the Fascists have not a worthwhile idea in baiting the Jews it will die anyway."[16]

If this broadside was not enough to kill the bill, Glass soon learned that Hepburn was cool to the idea. The bill was already prepared and entered on the Order Paper of the legislature when its sponsor was stopped in the corridor by the premier and advised that government legal counsel were doubtful of its constitutionality. Still Glass did not concede. He conducted a private canvass of constitutional experts and only when they confirmed that the bill probably trenched upon federal powers did he abandon the idea.[17] The unresolved problem was that no federal criminal law existed to curb the masses of hate propaganda in circulation.

Meanwhile the federal government was resisting demands from the Trades and Labour Council and other concerned groups for a probe of fascist and Nazi activities in Canada. Early in December 1937, Justice Minister Lapointe announced that the fascists were under surveillance but he declined to institute an inquiry on the grounds that the publicity would serve to encourage subversive elements. However, investigative journalism was already in action, and the result was to bear out Lapointe's opinion. Ironically, it was Rabbi Eisendrath who touched off the publicity by a statement that the Nazis were putting pressure on naturalized Germans in Kitchener to support their activities, on peril of reprisals against relatives in Germany. The *Globe and Mail* assigned a reporter to investigate, and ran a series of articles that attracted widespread attention. The Canadian public learned that a Nazi organization, the Deutsche Bund, was working among Canadians of German descent, albeit with limited success; that its official organ, the *Deutsche Zeitung*, carried innocuous advertisements offering information which, on reply, brought forth packages of the most vicious anti-semitic material. Moreover it came to light that Canadian fascist groups were distributing vast quantities of Nazi propaganda. Literature in both French and English poured out of Germany to their headquarters and was then offered free of charge to readers of *Le Fasciste Canadien* or *The Thunderbolt*. These two publications themselves were found to be spreading the most anti-democratic, as well anti-semitic, propaganda. The CUF organ called for control of the press, nationalization of resources, abolition of provincial administrations, and establishment of a corporate state. All liberals and leftists were referred to as "the scum front." Its staple theme, of course, was "international Jewish finance." As well as offering German material, *The Thunderbolt* solicited subscribers for the Mosley papers, *Action* and *The Blackshirt*.[18]

This exposé of the workings of Nazi propaganda in Canada focused attention upon the leader of the major fascist organization, Adrien Arcand, who was introduced to *Globe and Mail* readers as "the brilliant young French Canadian."[19] Until now Arcand was virtually unknown outside Quebec; but the *Globe* articles, combined with his own arresting claim of eighty thousand members, made him a national figure. The *Globe* sent one of its top reporters to Montreal to interview him; a two-part series appeared in *Maclean's* magazine; and David Griffin of the *Toronto Star* spent a day with the Arcand family. This first wave of publicity was followed by articles in American magazines, including *The Nation* and even the intellectual journal *Foreign Affairs*. The ultimate accolade came a few months later when *Life* did a picture story on Arcand and his movement.

The would-be Canadian Fuehrer was depicted as a "tall, good-looking . . . slim, clean-shaven" young man resembling Mosley but acting like Hitler with his "pyrotechnic oratory." Frederick Edwards in *Maclean's* ambivalently described him as "a zealot . . . a fanatic but no fool . . . truculent, with a chip on his shoulder . . . no sense of humour . . . courage[ous], reckless, sincere . . . a passionate fighter." The image Arcand projected at this stage was that of a charismatic leader, able to elicit the adoration of his followers. "I would die for him," Major Scott, the drill-master, was quoted as saying, "so would every man in the party ."[20] Arcand appeared to be the stuff that dictators were made of; as one of his interviewers put it, "ripe material to foment and lead such fascist or Nazi movements as tolerant and usually good-natured Canadians will stand for."[21]

Not only the physical but the ideological man took shape from all the publicity. Foremost among his ideas, which were a composite of Mosley's, Hitler's and Mussolini's, was his "persistent and often vicious anti-semitism." He would deprive Jews of citizenship rights, leaving them only "negative rights"—a concept which he variously interpreted. (A complete racist, he would also disenfranchise Negroes and Asiatics.) He blamed the Jews for the Depression and predicted another serious downturn in 1941: a Mosley theme, reflecting awareness that economic crisis was the best climate for aspiring fascist movements. Naturally he identified the Jews with both communism and capitalism: "The Jew is everywhere. He has seized control of our gold, our pulp, our press. He controls our government." (At this his interviewer interjected, "Your statements about Jews are not believed by many people. It is a fact that there is not a single Jew on the board of directors of a single Canadian bank or mortgage company or of a single utility company or of the rail or ocean transportation companies.")[22] In Arcand's scheme of things, the 150,000 Jews in Canada would ultimately be expelled.

Hoping to duplicate Hitler's rise to power, he declared that he would take over the country by constitutional means, reserving his revolution for afterwards. (Mosley also stressed power by the vote alone.) Arcand told the *Star's* David Griffin that although he was ready now, with a shadow cabinet in the wings, he preferred to wait three years and be voted in. But once elected, he would destroy the party system and organize a corporate state. Like Mussolini, he would retain the capitalistic system but place it under government control. The newly published party regulations gave the details of a structure copied from Italian and British corporative theory. There was a Grand Council selected by the leader, with various corporations of professionals, industrialists and technicians to act as advisors. These corporations would have to await the accession to power; but a corporation of writers and orators was already in action, identifiable by the red felt 'P' for Propagandist on their blue shirts. In addition, there were the legions—the muscle of the party. The organization was pyramidal, with councils at various levels (provincial, county, municipal, zone, ward groups and sections), each council nominated by the one above, with the provincial members chosen by the Grand Council . Like its European models, Arcand's movement rested on the leadership principle; according to the official rule book, "the Leader of the Party is the Supreme Authority."[23]

Appropriating such sentiments as patriotism, godliness, the sanctity of the family, and free enterprise, Arcand aimed to attract conservative elements. His violent anti-communism and his law and order statements, reminiscent of Mussolini in 1920–22, placed him on common ground with more respectable company. Certainly the Canadian Legion could not have objected to his statement that "we will fight for our King, our God and our country. Communism is a crime against God, the family, the King, the home, everything. They want to destroy all that."[24] Nor would the Canadian Manufacturers' Association have disapproved of such sentiments as " our organization stands for God, family, private property and personal initiative."[25] Actually there were two fascist party lines, one for Quebec and one for the rest of the country. Arcand reserved his talk of loyalty to the gracious sovereign and respect for the British North America Act for English-speaking Canada. In French Canada, he was full of nationalistic rhetoric of the Abbé Groulx school.

Nevertheless, his nation-wide ambitions would not permit him to follow the extreme nationalists into the contemporary dream of Laurentia, an independent French-Canadian state. No matter how he tried to play down his anti-separatist position in Quebec, it placed him on the defensive. Similarly, his imperialist stand —another concession to English Canada—took a lot of explaining in his home province. Catering to both language groups confronted Arcand with all the traditional difficulties of national politics in Canada.

While admitting to great admiration for Hitler and Mussolini, he consistently denied that his movement received any foreign aid. He was not generally believed. Rumours were current that he was in the pay of the Nazis. Certainly this charge was made by all the leftist groups, united since 1935 in the Popular Front. For example, A.A. MacLeod, chairman of the League for Peace and Democracy, claimed that the Canadian fascists received salaries from one of Hitler's agents in this country, whom he described as the head of a German firm.[26] The communist Fred Rose was more explicit. In a pamphlet published in 1938, he charged that the paymaster-agent was the Toronto head of the Fischer Ball Bearing Company.[27] In a book published in 1941, Professor Watson Kirkconnell repeated the earlier rumours: "German funds financed the organization [i.e. Arcand's], the pay-off contact in Montreal being the North German Lloyd Steamship Company and in Toronto the Fischer Aktiongesellschaft, in the Terminal Warehouse."[28] Lending substance to these allegations is the fact that an executive of the Fischer Ball Bearing Company was interned with Arcand in 1940.

In the early months of 1938 there were portents that it might indeed be the year of the fascists, as Arcand boasted. The Ontario press carried pictures of fascist "legionnaires" drilling in Montreal, and a shaven-headed Major Scott (looking like Mussolini's double) giving the Nazi salute against a background of a huge swastika wreathed in maple leaves. These pictures were accompanied by alarming headlines such as "Quebec Fascists Aim to Raise Eight Divisions Under Leadership of Former Canadian Army Officers."[29] Then came a disturbing news item that the new mayor of Sorel, Quebec, and two aldermen had publicly announced that they were fascists. Moreover, when Arcand held a rally at Sorel to capitalize on this conquest, three mayors from neighbouring towns also appeared on his platform.[30] (The mayor of Sorel was presented with a mirror engraved with the fascist emblem, which he promised to hang in his office.)* This event was followed almost immediately by the court victory of Arcand's chief aide, Dr. Lambert.

So far Lapointe had managed to withstand demands for a probe, but when J. S. Woodsworth waved a picture of drilling Quebec fascists before the House, he capitulated. Pointing out that military drilling by unauthorized groups was a criminal offence liable to prosecution by provincial authorities, Lapointe implicitly conceded that Duplessis would never act. He then announced that since a political group was involved, the federal government would step in and investigate and possibly take action. He added, however, that not only Quebec fascists but those in Ontario and Manitoba would come under investigation since it was understood that they were all associated.[31]

Reaction to the announcement of the probe was varied. Duplessis belittled the alleged fascist menace as a communist-inspired rumour. The League for Peace and Democracy commended the government's action and, as if to disprove its reputation as a communist-front organization, asked that the inquiry also look at the influence of communists in the labour movement. The Canadian Jewish Congress was skeptical about the whole thing. According to

---

*In the files of the Canadian Jewish Congress there is a notarized document from Alphonse Bourret, mayor of Sorel, signed March 7, 1938, denying that he or his council was fascist. However there does not appear to have been a public retraction.

its officials, Ottawa had had detailed reports of the fascist movement for months, and the probe would not reveal anything that was not already known. The *Globe and Mail* summed up the grounds for skepticism: "The fact that the movement flourishes in Quebec province is regarded as sufficient reason why the federal government will not take any action that may affect them adversely in the political sense, according to anti-fascists."[32]

Arcand's own response was to take the offensive. He immediately wrote to Lapointe, demanding a royal commission on government corruption[33] and, in an interview with the *Toronto Star*, he exploded with wrath. "We will march to Ottawa and show the Honorable Ernest Lapointe what we are. We will not stop drilling. Our organization goes forward."

"Do you seriously mean you would descend on Ottawa with a fascist regiment?" the reporter asked.

"I do, and they would be better drilled and in better order than the soldiers they have there now."[34]

Soon after this emotional outburst, Arcand reverted to his usual constitutional position. "We will not march on Ottawa," he stated. "When we go we will go as M.P.'s in Pullman cars."[35]

Indeed, Arcand now announced that the fascists had formed a national party and would contest seats in the next federal election. The new party was based on a merger of his own party in Quebec with Whittaker's Canadian Nationalist Party in the West and a newly organized Ontario group. They would shortly hold a national convention to choose a Supreme Chief. In the meantime, he would unveil the Ontario leader the following week.

It was not John Ross Taylor who emerged from the fanfare as leader of the Ontario fascists. He and the Canadian Union of Fascists, with whom he had now merged his few followers, appear to have been pushed aside in favour of another local group calling itself the Nationalist Party. The previous November Arcand had heralded the formation of this group with an editorial in *Le Fasciste Canadien* headed "Welcome Ontario." Actually the group had had a long underground existence going back to the Swastika Clubs of the East End Beaches. Its leader, Joseph C. Farr, had played an active role in the anti-semitic disturbances of 1933. In 1938 Farr was selling beverages, his involvement with the Nationalist Party having already cost him at least one job.[36] The paramilitary aspect of fascism held an irresistible appeal for him, although hitherto his "campaigns" had consisted of driving Jewish bathers off the public beaches. This was the Ontario leader Arcand introduced at the beginning of March.

Now that fascism had "gone national," it had become a genuine cause for concern in Canada. To Arcand's extravagant membership claims, Farr added his own of ten thousand paid-up members in Ontario. They gave equally exaggerated predictions for electoral success. Many people began to look at Arcand and his growing organization and to ask, with *Maclean's* author Frederick Edwards, "Will this movement turn Canada from a democracy to a totalitarian state or is it just an ephemeral outbreak of anti-semitism?"

X A National Convention

At precisely the same time as Arcand was announcing the merger of the fascist groups in Canada, a far more world-shattering *anschluss* took place. In March 1938 Hitler took over Austria; this act of aggression brought to a close the short period which has been referred to as his "respectable years." When his designs on Czechoslovakia became obvious a month or so later, most thinking Canadians realized that Nazism was not just a nationalist movement, but a relentless expansionism aimed at world domination. While Canada continued to support Chamberlain's policy of appeasement, Hitler was henceforth recognized as an international menace.

The *anschluss* had tremendous repercussions on Arcand and the future of the Canadian fascist movement. When Canadian public opinion hardened against Hitler, it also turned decisively against his imitators at home. Writing in *Maclean's* shortly after the Austrian take-over, Frederick Edwards concluded that "Hitler quashed Canadian fascism's hopes of becoming a political power this summer." In this article, written at the end of March, he dramatically reversed his earlier assessment of Arcand's movement as a growing force in Canada, speaking now of "the new party, if it still exists when this gets into print."[1]

Thus it was not an auspicious beginning for Arcand's Ontario campaign. Continuing the Mosley tactics of provocation, Arcand and Farr scheduled their first meetings in April in the Jewish district of Toronto and provoked the predictable counter-demonstrations. With the fascists safely ensconced inside the meeting hall, police disciplinary action fell entirely on the heads of the anti-fascist street demonstrators. As in England, this led to charges of police bias in favour of the fascists. For example, early in June, police were battling three hundred anti-fascists who were trying to stop a shirt group meeting.[2] A few days later, the police were again in the position of protecting fascists, patrolling the street in front of their meeting hall and dispersing demonstrators. Moreover, the anti-fascists claimed that when two of their young men attempted to enter the hall, they were beaten while police looked on.[3] The situation was reversed another time, with the fascists under seige by fifteen hundred vociferous antagonists and afraid to venture out of their meeting hall. But those arrested were invariably from the ranks of the anti-fascists.

If there was some police animus against the demonstrators, it was attributable to the fact that communists, Trotskyites and anarchists had assumed the leadership of the anti-fascist forces. Both the Montreal and Toronto police were obsessively concerned with these elements, to the exclusion of anything beyond a perfunctory surveillance of fascists. Mayor Raynault of Montreal and his chief of police admitted they were so busy stamping out Reds that they left the fascists alone.[4] In Toronto, Chief Draper continued his witch-hunt with a police probe of local communists. Draper's so-called "Red Squad" which conducted the investigation was highly suspect in the eyes of the left-wing groups. A communist alderman charged that one of the detectives was himself a member of the fascist party,[5] and an activist of those days recalls that this same detective and another on the special squad were "always at the *Casa d'Italia*."[6] Unquestionably the police regarded communists as a greater threat to law and order than fascists; thus the identification of anti-fascists with communists militated against a genuine effort on the part of the police to contain fascist activities.

Public opinion and the press, however, reflected greatly increased hostility towards the home-grown Nazis. When Arcand spoke in Toronto he was no longer described as "brilliant" and "handsome" but as a "tall, gaunt Blackshirt."[7] And indignation over his frequent public appearances was compounded by the fact that fascists were now known to be drilling in Ontario. This was Farr's contribution to the movement. Although his efforts to organize the Ontario Nationalist Party were reputedly lagging, he had managed to enlist a corps of "legionnaires" who marched and drilled under his instruction several times a week. A sergeant-major in spirit long after he was mustered out of the British army, Farr relished these toy soldier exercises. A newspaper photograph shows him with a dozen legionnaires, some of an age to have served in the war, all Anglo-Saxons except for one Italian and a Dutch immigrant who had recently come to Ontario by way of the United States. Wearing blue shirts and swastika arm bands, they went through their paces in rented halls; but notwithstanding Farr's injunction to wear their fascist uniforms openly, once outside they shed them and reverted to their everyday lives. Farr's leadership qualities did not extend beyond those of a drill-master. A follower not a leader, he was certainly not the man to counteract the anti-Nazi temper of the times. [8]

Meanwhile the party was running into problems in Quebec. The papacy had denounced Hitler for breaking the Concordat of 1933 and, as a result, the Quebec clergy had become very anti-Nazi. Yet Arcand had continued to be pro-Hitler. This had gradually estranged the parish priests from him, many of whom had been his supporters. His equivocal position on this issue, and its consequences, are indicated in this portion of an interview with David Martin which appeared in *The Nation* in February 1938.

"What stand do you take on the conflict between the Nazis and the Vatican?"

"That is very far from here. We do not mingle in it."

"You do not support the Catholic church against the Nazis?"

Once again Arcand hesitated. "From this distance it is difficult to take a stand. We receive contradictory reports."

"I have heard," I persisted, "that your sympathy for the Nazi regime and your failure to support the Vatican against Hitler has resulted in the alienation of a considerable section of the Catholic church that formerly was sympathetic to you. The Catholic church in Quebec still stands for corporatism and is sympathetic to fascism, but is opposed to your movement for that reason."

"The Catholic church is not fascist," insisted Arcand. "It stands for corporatism." It was obvious that I had touched a sore spot. Arcand paused before he completed his reply. "There are a number, a very small number in the church who support us. But for each one who does there are at least two who are opposed."

The abandonment by the clergy was a sore blow to his hopes. Indeed, a hostile French-Canadian editor suggested that Arcand's move into Ontario was an attempt to recoup his losses in Quebec.[9]

A second blow to the prosperity of the National Social Christian Party occurred in May 1938, when eleven members, including Lambert and Lessard, left the party. Their "sensational retreat" (as one French-language paper called it)[10] was the culmination of the dissension that had surfaced the year before with the revolt of the younger members. The trouble was that Arcand wanted to be Hitler while his party wanted him to be Mussolini. Apparently, he had been ruling alone since March, with the help of a wealthy relative, Hugues Clement. The dissidents, led by Lambert, protested against supreme authority being vested in one man, claiming that it was contrary to the party constitution. They wanted the movement to follow the Italian fascist model. As Lambert explained to a reporter, "Fascism in Italy is not bossed by Mussolini, because the country is governed by the fascist Grand Council." He added ingenuously, "If our party were in power I wouldn't dare talk to you like this. I'd be shot. Just as well to get this over with now before we go into power."[11] But the party was to meet its destiny without him. In a stern communiqué, Arcand officially expelled Lambert, Lessard and the other nine for "insubordination, violation of rules, and insurrection against the structure of the party."[12] Although Lambert and Lessard tried to rally support for choosing another leader, Arcand weathered the revolt. Eventually five of the eleven defectors were reinstated and the breach was papered over. Nevertheless, the split in the party was a serious one.

In any event, public suspicion of Arcand and his followers was sharply increased in the spring of 1938 by a spy scare and by repeated charges that the fascists were importing arms. The spy scare was triggered when R.B. Bennett charged in the House of Commons that a "Nazi emissary" was operating in Canada. This was corroborated by Toronto police who declared that paid agents were in the country organizing German- and English-speaking groups into Nazi forces.[13] A few days later, Bennett's mystery man was revealed as Dr. Gerhardt, the dapper German who had set up the Deutsche Bund in Canada. It was rumoured that, in between his Canadian tours of duty, Gerhardt acted as a personal aide to Hitler, accompanying him, as recently as May, on the official visit to Rome. This dubious character, on whom the RCMP had kept a file since 1934, was also said to have become a naturalized Canadian; but the government managed to side-step this question when it was raised in the House.[14] Bennett's charges were made against a background of the highly publicized U.S. Dies Committee's investigation into un-American activities. One of the revelations from across the border was that the Nazi spy ring uncovered in the United States was also at work in Montreal. This much the public heard. There would have been more alarm had a certain memorandum, now in the National Defence Records in the Public Archives, been leaked. Dated June 11, 1938, and marked "Most Secret," it emanated from the office of the Chief of Staff and was addressed to all District Military Officers. It informed them that "recent evidence" disclosed "the definite existence in Canada of a German espionage organization," whose instructions were to transmit to Japan information obtained from spying on industrial plants.

Less well founded were the constant rumours about smuggling of arms by Quebec fascists. It was reported that five hundred Smith and Wesson revolvers had come in from the United States for Arcand's legionnaires. These rumours were only partially laid to rest when Lapointe told the House of Commons at the end of June that an RCMP investigation had found that the Montreal fascists had no arms.[15]

All these factors—Hitler's aggression, the marching and drilling of local fascists, the rumours of subversion—ensured that Arcand received a poor reception when he tried to arrange for a national fascist convention. Initially, he had thought to hold it in Kingston, but when the mayor flatly declared that there would be no parade permit and that "the citizens of Kingston do not extend a hand of welcome to this proposed convention,"[16] he announced his intention of going to Toronto. There the opposition was equally strong but less prohibitive, the mayor taking the position that he could not stop the convention but urging private interests to refuse to rent space for it.[17] Meanwhile Arcand and Farr were holding public meetings in Toronto, mainly in the heavily ethnic districts, in a deliberate attempt to incite the anti-fascists and thus gain publicity for the movement.

But the fascists achieved their greatest shock value when a *Toronto Star* photograph appeared showing four militiamen, in the uniform of the Royal Canadian Artillery, sitting in the front row at a meeting of the Ontario Nationalist Party. According to the story, the gunners (admittedly members of the fascist party) went to the meeting after drill practice at a nearby barracks, marched to the front of the hall and saluted Arcand while the audience of three hundred and forty cheered. The *Star* picture created a sensation. The matter was raised in the House and the Minister of Defence, Ian Mackenzie, promised an investigation.

Farr hinted at other fascist militiamen. "Perhaps there may be many more soldiers on our list who [will] appear at future meetings," he told a reporter,[18] thus lending credence to a common report that the fascists were spreading propaganda in the militia and the army. The incident of the fascist gunners had its American counterpart. Almost at the same time, four army and navy officers were caught attending a Nazi rally in Philadelphia. In Canada, as in other countries, the military was well represented among the fascist element. Indeed, the participation of soldiers and policemen in the fascist movement was common knowledge. On March 31, 1938, the *Globe and Mail* wrote: "It is reported a number of soldiers are members of Arcand's party, as well as several Montreal policemen." And in April the Anglican bishop of Montreal, J.C. Farthing, warned that "fascist legions are being drilled by Canadian officers who served overseas." War veterans attended a fascist meeting in Verdun in May. And one of Farr's right-hand men was discovered to be an active member of the Canadian Corps Association. There were even hints that the Corps leadership flirted with the fascists at one point; the general manager of the Corps reunion admitted that he had met with Arcand and other fascists in Montreal.[19]

The paramilitary character of the fascist groups and their emphasis on law and order held considerable appeal for the military mind. Veterans' organizations were seduced by the anti-communist propaganda of the fascists and misled by their patriotic and imperialist talk. The Ontario Nationalist Party, recognizing this, adopted Whittaker's formula even to the name, and presented fascism in the guise of nationalism. Like Whittaker, Farr also played upon the social and economic discontent of the veterans.

By the summer of 1938, however, most ex-soldiers and militiamen realized that fascism was as much a threat to their conservative values as communism. They saw that the fascists' pledge of loyalty to king and country was quite a different affair from their own. By the time of the fascist convention in July, they had turned back to more acceptable paths of patriotism. Indeed, the veterans' organizations took the lead in alerting the country to the dangers represented by Arcand. In Kingston the Canadian Legion strongly supported the city council's refusal to permit a fascist parade. In Sudbury, an offshoot of the Legion denounced fascists equally with communists. The most vocal denunciation of the fascists by a veterans' organization came from the Canadian Corps Association. It happened over the choosing of a new emblem by the fascists. Realizing that Hitler had fallen into very ill repute in Canada, Arcand attempted to give his party a new image free from Nazi associations. In place of the swastika, which the party had used since its inception, he substituted a flaming torch not unlike the emblem of the Canadian Corps Association. At the same time, he discarded the National Socialist name of the Quebec party and announced that the dominion-wide organization, then in formation, would be known as the National Unity Party. Irate over the fascists appropriating the flaming torch emblem, the president of the Canadian Corps fulminated, "Stealing names and labels as a camouflage for subversive 'isms' is a trick that fools nobody."[20]

Meanwhile, in the West feeling was growing that something had to be done about *their* fascists. Although Whittaker was old and sick and was to die that autumn, the Canadian Nationalist Party was still active in Manitoba and Saskatchewan. So much so that the Attorney General of Saskatchewan, T.C. Davis, wrote to Lapointe on March 29, 1938, suggesting that the government should consider amending the Criminal Code to cover group libel. "In a country such as this where we have a highly mixed population, particularly in Western Canada, a movement of this type serves no good purpose and merely breeds a lot of ill will," he wrote. There was nothing in the present law to control these Hitler-style groups, whose aim was to exterminate Jews and Freemasons, and "it might be advisable to amend the Criminal Code as proposed by Luchkovitch, then M.P. for Edmonton."²¹ (In 1935, the Ukrainian Michael Luchkovitch, angered at a slur against his people by a sitting judge, tried to get the House of Commons to pass legislation prohibiting defamation of persons or groups on account of race, colour or religion. His bill did not reach second reading.) Davis added that personally he doubted the effectiveness of this type of legislation; nevertheless, his letter testifies to his concern over the problem.

Lapointe, however, did not believe that legislation was called for. On June 28, 1938, during a Commons debate on subversive elements at work in the country, he gave his assessment of the Canadian fascist movement. In the first place, he said, the fascists did not pose a real danger in Canada. He confided that he had considered passing a law like Great Britain's Public Order Act of 1936, prohibiting political processions in uniform, but had come to the conclusion that this would give unwarranted importance to the fascists. As to the strength of their movement, they boasted of thousands of followers when in effect they were only a handful. Both the communists and fascists only sought publicity and he warned that people who took them seriously played into their hands. To set the example, he introduced a little humour by quoting a fascist as saying that if his party took power, "the first Jew to be expelled would be Ernest Lapointe."

This official view of the fascists on the eve of their national convention was probably correct as far as it went. Card-carrying members numbered only a few thousand. At the time of his defection in May, Lambert estimated there were eighteen hundred paid-up members in Quebec. In Ontario, police files showed an active list of about a thousand. Public opinion, too, was undoubtedly mustered against Nazi and Italian fascist ideologies. Nevertheless, Canadian fascists had one trump card: anti-semitism. The success or failure of the convention scheduled for July 4 in Toronto would largely depend on the level of popular feeling against the Jews. To one Toronto clergyman it appeared to be high. Writing to the *Globe and Mail* on June 20, the Reverend Gordon Domm of Bathurst United Church stated bluntly: "There is probably enough anti-semitism dormant among Canadians of all ranks which, if the stage is thus cleverly set, can threaten our whole land. Verily, it can happen here."

The national fascist convention was preceded by a secret session in Kingston, for which the authorities stood ready. Five Mounties in civilian dress were in town to assist local and provincial police; but since the fascists were in hiding the policemen had nothing to do. After their mysterious sojourn in Kingston, the fascists motored to Toronto and checked into a hotel on Sherbourne Street. There Arcand gave a press conference. Announcing the party's change of name and emblem, he disclosed that he himself had been chosen national leader and he named his associates from across Canada who were with him. The party platform, as outlined, was clearly an attempt to make fascism palatable to Canadians. National unity and other widely acceptable values were played up while anti-semitism was disguised behind code words (although Arcand openly stated that only Gentiles would be accepted as members). Symptomatic of their desire for respectability, the fascist chiefs sent a telegram to the Governor General pledging their loyalty.

With all the advance publicity which the fascist convention had received, most Torontonians were aware that an event of some significance was taking place on July 4, 1938. As well as the main event, protest meetings were scheduled at various places and the police were on the alert for trouble. Arcand's predictions for an overwhelming success were carried in all the papers and no one really knew what to expect.

That evening hundreds of people filed into the dignified brown interior of Massey Hall for the National Unity Party convention. Estimates of the crowd vary from *Life* magazine's fifteen hundred to the *Globe and Mail's* probably over-generous twenty-five hundred, but undoubtedly it was a large meeting. As the audience waited for the speeches to begin, dozens of Blueshirts paced up and down the aisles, swaggering like their Nazi prototypes. As he usually did on these occasions, Arcand tried to employ mass psychology. Before making his dramatic entry, he had his auxiliaries warm up the audience; that evening the first speaker was the man he had recently named leader of the Ontario party, Joseph Farr. An unprepossessing figure, Farr nevertheless evoked enthusiastic applause for his gibes at the Jewish race. When he sat down, leaders from other provinces spoke. Most were young men. One youthful fascist dramatically labelled democracy "a reeking carcass hot from the ghettos of Europe. " The audience was now sufficiently prepared for the man whom the previous speaker lauded as "our inspiring leader." Escorted by a guard of Blueshirts, Arcand marched to the stage. On this occasion his platform style—a well-studied copy of Hitler's strident shouting and arm-flailing—was somewhat more restrained, as he always toned down for English-speaking audiences. The speech itself was a tirade against democracy and Jews. Audience reaction is difficult to gauge because eye-witness reports differed so markedly. *The Globe and Mail* recorded "thunderous applause" while the *Toronto Star* reporter observed that Arcand's listeners walked out in droves.

Outside Massey Hall anti-fascists milled angrily. Urged on by some fiery communists and anarchists, a street demonstration a block away was about to march on Massey Hall when it was broken up by police. The size of the street gathering was also variously reported: four hundred according to the *Star* but twice that number in the *Globe*'s opinion. After the police arrested four known communists, the protesters detoured to a nearby Labour Temple.

The evening's largest meeting was a huge protest rally at Maple Leaf Gardens, organized by the League for Peace and Democracy. Although the League's leadership had been infiltrated by communists, its active members included liberals, intellectuals and idealists and its public meetings drew ordinary men and women united by a common desire to stand up against current threats to democracy. Alarmed at the presence of a Nazi-style rally in their city, ten thousand people were seated on the wooden benches of the hockey auditorium. The principal speaker was William E. Dodd, the former American ambassador to Germany, whose message was a warning to the democractic countries to cooperate before it was too late. The most forceful speaker was R.L. Calder, the nationally known spokesman for civil liberties from Montreal. "With authoritarian and non-parliamentary government as their objective," he told his audience, "there are men not far from here tonight who, whatever they say, have violence in their hearts. They are trying to captivate [sic] the army and bring about civil war." He hinted that the fascists were backed by important men. Another speaker claimcd that Arcand's party was subsidized by Germany and was just a cover for Nazi espionage.

Yet another protest rally, this one sponsored by the CCF, was being held on the lawn of the provincial legislature at Queen's

Park. According to the chairman, William Dennison (a future mayor of the city), the meeting's purpose was to present a social and labour alternative to fascism and, incidentally, to keep their people away from trouble with the fascists. The mild-mannered Dennison probably startled at least some of his five hundred or so listeners lounging on the smoothly clipped lawn with his assertions that Nazi agents were working through the fascists to undermine the country. Citing a counter-espionage agent as his source, he charged that the fascists were armed, and that the German consulate was putting pressure on German Canadians to engage in subversive activity.

After the night of the fascist convention, many people wondered just how successful Arcand had been. News coverage was extremely wide and certainly afforded the fascists the publicity they sought. Probably the greatest recognition of the movement was the picture spread in *Life* which appeared shortly after the convention —a photographer had earlier been despatched to Montreal where Arcand's wealthy cousin, Hugues Clement, had chauffeured him around.[22] Pictures of drilling legionnaires and worshipful followers of the "Canadian Fuehrer" illustrated the feature's theme that "Fascism in Canada has become a menacing problem within the past year." But having stated that Arcand edited the official paper of the premier of Quebec and that he was treated with "benign tolerance " by the premier of Ontario, *Life* concluded that fascism was still "a minor matter" in the dominion to the north. The Quebec papers were generally unimpressed with the Toronto fascist rally, although *Le Devoir* used an uncharacteristically respectful tone in speaking of "Monsieur Arcand." Only Arcand's own sheet, *Le Combat National*, dubbed it "a triumphal debut." As for the Toronto papers, they might have been covering different events. The *Globe* saw the convention as much larger, much better received and, on the whole, more successful than did the *Star*.

Whatever Arcand's real success, he had far outdistanced his nearest rivals, the Canadian Union of Fascists. A few days before the Blueshirts' convention, the Blackshirts had held a meeting in a working-class district in Toronto's west end. Perhaps they had hoped to benefit by the publicity Arcand was receiving; in any event, they, too, had press coverage and police surveillance. But the CUF was badly in decline. Only about thirty faithful had turned up to hear speakers proclaim that Canada was controlled by Jewish financiers and that parliamentary government was in the last stages of consumption. The unspoken enemy, however, was Arcand. "We were here long before him," the chairman explained to a reporter. One member pinpointed the reason for the Blackshirts' poor showing compared with the Blueshirts when he wistfully expressed the group's need for "a gallant leader." Undoubtedly, Arcand's main strength lay in his impressive, if imitative, "fuehrer" image.

Retreat to Quebec

The Toronto convention marked the peak of Arcand's career. After that he faded rapidly as a national figure. The summer of 1938 was too late for a Nazi-style movement of national scope in Canada. The German occupation of Austria had been followed almost immediately by Hitler's demands on the Sudetenland district of Czechoslovakia. War in Europe appeared imminent, and if it came there was little doubt that Canada would be drawn in. In this climate, a tolerant nation was fast losing patience with subversive elements in its midst.

Nevertheless there were two factors which kept Canadian fascism alive. One was the increased activity of Nazi organizers at work among the German-speaking population in the West. Often working behind the front of a Canadian fascist group, they were attempting to build up a "fifth column" to undermine the national unity so essential in the event of war. The second factor was the strong anti-war sentiment in French Canada. Forsaking the imperialist doctrine of his party program, Arcand appealed to the isolationism of his compatriots. It marked his retreat from the national to the provincial scene.

The Nazi campaign in western Canada was directed by the German consulate with the assistance of professional Bundists like the *Deutsche Zeitung's* editor, Bernard Bott. Almost every prairie town with a substantial German population was said to have a branch of the Deutsche Bund.[1] And while Bott's paper had formerly discouraged German participation in the Canadian Nationalist Party,[2] the new policy was clearly one of cooperation with the Canadian fascists. Often the local Bund and the local fascist group had the same personnel; Hans Fries was an example of a man who wore two hats. Since coming to Canada from Hitler's Munich in 1930, Fries had farmed at several locations in Saskatchewan; in fact, however, he was an organizer for the Bund. At the same time, he worked openly for the Canadian fascist movement. Just how openly can be seen from a letter he wrote to the editor of the Regina *Leader-Post*, commenting on an anti-fascist editorial in the Saskatoon *Star Phoenix* entitled "It Is Happening Here." Fascism, Fries declared, was not a party; it was a movement which came into the field wherever communism appeared. Fascism stood for nationalism and combatted the internationalism of the Jewish "parasites" who kept workers embroiled in strikes and riots. The letter closed off with the fascist slogan: "Canada for Canadians." [3]

Fries worked with another Nazi organizer from Regina, who called himself the western secretary of the fascists. Together they travelled to farming communities making speeches and organizing fascist groups. They claimed to have three to four thousand followers in the province, with local branches in all German and Ukrainian districts. Their parent body was apparently the Canadian Union of Fascists since, according to the *Star Phoenix*, they were hoping to have everything in readiness for an autumn visit of Ross Taylor, the national organizer from Toronto. (After his short and unhappy association with Arcand, Taylor had become active in the CUF.) In the opinion of the *Star Phoenix*, it was the Saskatchewan fascists' "ultimate objective to appeal to Hitler for protection of the German minorities here, although it is not clear what the German Canadians need protection against."[4] This strangely inapplicable transference to Canada of the Sudetenland situation, was also the gist of R.B. Bennett's sensational charges in the House of Commons on May 24:

> In this very country today there are emissaries of Germany—I say that on my responsibility as a member of this House —talking to minorities about their rights. A friend of mine in the legal profession was consulted on this matter by an old German; it is the younger ones, not the older ones who are swayed and moved by such appeals.[5]

Indeed Nazi and fascist activity in Saskatchewan was sufficiently alarming that a large protest meeting was held in June 1938 and a deluge of letters from veterans' groups and patriotic societies, expressing their concern, descended upon the Minister of Justice in Ottawa.[6] The situation continued to cause alarm. A year later a resident of a little town not far from Saskatoon reported to CCF headquarters that "this spring fascist activities here so menaced the peace of the community that the Canadian Legion found it necessary to organize a Protect Democracy drive."[7] Even after the outbreak of war, the M.P. for Prince Albert, John Diefenbaker, was asking the government what it intended to do about Nazi influence in Saskatchewan.[8]

While Saskatchewan with its large German population attracted Nazi activity, its neighbouring provinces were experiencing similar problems. In Manitoba the Deutsche Bund was extremely active, especially in Winnipeg which was its western headquarters. The Bund often worked through the Canadian Nationalist Party, which (to quote a Jewish citizen of Winnipeg) was "still going strong."[9] Despite the anti-defamation legislation of 1934, its organ, *The Canadian Nationalist,* continued to print vicious libels, but the Jewish community, taking a reading of local sentiment, was reluctant to challenge it again in the courts. Pro-Nazi propaganda was widespread in the province. In April 1938 a Winkler merchant wrote to the Department of National Defence to complain of Nazi activity by Mennonites who had come to Canada since 1925. According to his letter, they were spreading Hitlerism and antagonizing the inhabitants, including the Old Mennonites.[10] In Alberta, subversive elements were so much to the fore that the Canadian Corps Association demanded the appointment of a royal commission.[11].

As war drew near, the Deutsche Bund was obviously striving to create a disunity by a country-wide propaganda offensive. Both in the United States and Canada, Bundist policy now was to join forces with local fascist groups. In 1938 the Montreal branch of the Bund was holding public meetings on any pretext. In fact, they became so frequent that the sole Jewish alderman, Max Seigler, complained to the Deputy Police Chief that "Nazis and Fascists were having too much their own way in our city."[12] The police official agreed, but explained that they were not illegal like Communist meetings. The historian Mason Wade states that "much Italian and German money was spent in Quebec with the aim of embarrassing Britain" and he avers that the German State Railways office in Montreal paid subsidies to some ultra nationalist publications.[13]

Certainly Arcand was in close touch with the German consulate. The Dies Committee on Un-American Activities later made public a letter from the German consul in Montreal, Dr. Eckner, to the German ambassador in Washington, reporting that Arcand had come to see him about getting hold of Nazi despatches for publication. "Mr. Arcand has promised me," he wrote, "that his paper will reproduce these German despatches without indicating the source." Similarly, World Service, the Nazi news agency, typically referred inquiries from interested Canadians to Arcand in Montreal or to Jean Tissot in Ottawa.[14] According to a man who infiltrated Arcand's movement in the late thirties (and wrote about it afterwards for the *Montreal Standard*) in the autumn of 1938, Arcand proudly announced to his followers that Hitler had named him chief of the fascist movement in North America. This "honour" was apparently conveyed to him by Nazi agents who visited him that fall.[15] It is probably true because similar approaches were made to a renegade leader in India, with the objective of softening the Commonwealth's resolve to come to the aid of the mother country.

It was not inappropriate, therefore, that from the summer of 1938 Arcand was treated as a subversive element and subjected to unofficial restraints. In the first place, he was allowed little or no publicity. The CBC refused him radio time and the Quebec press (with the exception of his own paper, *L'Illustration Nouvelle*) imposed a virtual censorship upon his activities. Secondly, he was unequivocally denounced by the Catholic hierarchy. Nevertheless, his movement was enjoying a renewed popular success in Quebec because of his vocal espousal of isolationism.

While English Canada was strongly in favour of appeasement and cheered Chamberlain's capitulation at Munich, it nevertheless was prepared, along with Mackenzie King, to enter the war at Britain's side if necessary. French Canada, however—isolationist and suspicious of British imperialism—was opposed to participation. Reacting to Quebec public opinion, Arcand now pursued a vehemently non-interventionist line. Addressing large crowds at Montreal's market-places and church halls and in the Laurentian towns, he ranted against intervention in Europe and lamented "the rumours of going to war for rotten democracy."[16] If he were in power, he said, such a course would not even be considered without a national referendum. Moreover, he would lower the voting age to eighteen so that those who would be called upon to do the fighting could vote against war.

He had taken a popular position. *L'Illustration Nouvelle* (which by default had exclusive coverage of these rallies) reported great ovations for the speaker. That there was an enthusiastic response is attested to by a neutral observer. John Hoare, a journalist who had lived abroad for some years, on his return to Canada heard so much about Arcand and the Quebec fascist movement that he decided to investigate. In an article for *Saturday Night* he described an Arcand meeting at St. Thomas Aquinas church hall in Montreal. The audience, which he estimated at about four hundred, overflowed into the street, and Arcand addressed them through loud-speakers. Evidently his meetings still followed the set pattern, with Blueshirts on stage and the usual preliminary speeches to warm up the audience for the leader. One of the opening speakers —a veritable personification of the fictional "Goglu"—was a large fellow talking the *patois* of the people who delighted the crowd with his heavy-handed, anti-semitic humour. Then Arcand entered, flanked by Blueshirts. To Hoare, an interested observer, he appeared "a spare man with a clean-cut head, cropped hair and dictator's eyes." In introducing him, the chairman evoked sustained cheers when he classed him with Hitler, Mussolini and Franco. Arcand began with an attack on the old political parties. *"Rouge* or *bleu,* it is the same thing," he said. They would lead Canada into war. For his part, he would not go, and if he were in power, there would be no war without a plebiscite. Then he moved on to another safe topic—unemployment, which he blamed on international Jewry. Rhyming off Jewish names, Arcand had the crowd roaring responses as in some strange litany. Although Hoare recognized that Arcand was preaching to the converted, he took away an impression of "distinct ability" and warned readers of *Saturday Night* that the Canadian fuehrer was not a man to be underestimated.[17]

Further confirmation of Arcand's strength in Quebec at this period comes from the *Montreal Standard* article, "I Belonged to Arcand's Party." According to its author, who infiltrated into higher party circles, membership in Montreal alone rose to four thousand in 1938–39. There were English members from Rosemount and Verdun and recruiting was highly successful in St. Hyacinthe and several other Laurentian towns. A women's section under Madame Arcand was designed to keep the wives happy while their husbands drilled and attended frequent meetings.

Arcand was not the only fascist at work in Quebec at this late hour. In the first place, there were the groups that had splintered off from his own. Although no longer closely associated with Arcand, Joseph Ménard had lost none of his fanaticism. The revival of *Le Patriote*, however, had been short-lived; it ended forever in March 1938, probably because of the withdrawal of Dr. Lalanne's financial support. Then there was Dr. Lambert, the chief aide of Arcand's middle period. Nursing a bitter hatred against his former leader, he was now trying to promote a new movement based on corporatism. But the impressive façade that had made him such an asset to Arcand had crumbled, and an acquaintance found him "aged, exceedingly nervous, much stouter and with black rings under his eyes."[18] A far more serious contender for Arcand's title as Quebec's leading fascist was Paul Bouchard. Director of the weekly, *La Nation*, Bouchard was a fiery advocate of French-Canadian separatism. He was also an ardent admirer of Mussolini, and his proposed "Free French State in America" had all the trappings of the corporate state. Arcand's rivalry with Bouchard, which may be seen as a competition between Italian and German fascist models, went back to 1936 when Bouchard began to attract a following.* Now having shed the imperialist ideas acquired from Mosley, as well as his own national aspirations, Arcand sounded very much like Bouchard doctrinally. Neither wanted war with the Axis countries and both were vigorously preaching non-intervention in Europe's struggles. The two groups remained rivals, however, and it was not the National Unity Party of Arcand but Social Credit with whom Bouchard linked forces. [19]

Bouchard's paper, *La Nation*, was almost as fanatically anti-semitic as *Le Fasciste Canadien*. Indeed, the intrepid executive secre-

---

*In the November 1936 issue of *Le Fasciste Canadien*, Arcand used the same ridiculing tactics on Bouchard as on an earlier rival, Chalifoux of the *Fédération des Clubs Ouvriers*.

tary of the Canadian Jewish Congress, H. M. Caiserman, once wrote to its editors about the "extraordinary experience" of reading their paper, which he likened to "an edition of Streicher." In particular, an August 1938 issue was totally devoted to "the terrible Jewish problem" and, apart from one article mildly favourable to the Jews, was composed of anti-semitic propaganda. But more deplorable was the appearance that same month of an article propagating the Protocols of Zion in an organ of the Catholic church, *La Semaine Religieuse*—even worse, the article was reprinted in *L'Action Catholique*.[20]

Indeed, anti-semitism was very much alive in Quebec and was given new animation by the burning question of the Jewish refugees. In the summer of 1938 the exodus of Jews and non-Aryans (part-Jewish Christians) from Germany, Austria and Czechoslovakia accelerated rapidly. Nazi persecution had entered its penultimate phase and its victims were looking everywhere for sanctuary. Feeling a sense of responsibility about their plight, the democractic nations convened a conference at Evian in France to discuss ways and means of resettling them in non-German lands. There was some suggestion that under-populated parts of the British Commonwealth like Canada should provide a refuge. The reaction in French Canada was one of undisguised opposition, and the nationalist press led by *Le Devoir* condemned the Evian plan out of hand. It did not help the case for Jewish immigration that Henri Bourassa, touring Europe that summer, had conceived an unmistakable admiration for Hitler. In a series of articles which he wrote for *Le Devoir* he gave his "Impressions of Europe in 1938": in effect, an apologia for Nazi aggression in Czechoslovakia. In the July 28 issue, he maintained that Hitler had the right to take over the Slavic states because only he could create order out of chaos; and furthermore, if Hitler wanted to take Czechoslovakia in his eastward drive, France and Britain had no right to stop him. Notwithstanding, Bourassa gave his opinion that Hitler would never invade Czechoslovakia because its inhabitants were not of pure German stock.

The problem of sanctuary for the refugees became acute with the November pogroms in Germany, the so-called "Crystal Night," named for the smashed glass from Jewish businesses and homes that littered the streets of Berlin. Within a few days of this new tragedy, the British government announced that it would explore the possibilities of settling some of the expected surge of refugees in various colonies. Fearful that Canada might be asked to participate in some resettlement scheme, the nationalistic St. Jean-Baptiste Society in Quebec City began circulating a petition "protest[ing] vigorously against immigration of any kind whatever and especially against Jewish immigration." Ultimately 127,364 people signed the petition which was presented to the House of Commons early in 1939 by a Liberal member from Quebec, Wilfrid LaCroix. This solid block of opinion went unopposed as the voice of French Canada.

Although English and French Canada diverged on the question of participation in the impending war, they were in accord regarding the refugee question. By and large, the English-speaking provinces were opposed to any Jewish immigration; nevertheless, unlike Quebec, they were awash with sympathy for the refugees. The Protestant churches prayed for them while community leaders denounced the Nazis for their "bestial and shocking persecution of a helpless minority." A refugee committee was formed under the chairmanship of Sir Robert Falconer and Senator Cairine Wilson.* Protest rallies were held, notably an enormous one at Maple Leaf Gardens with the retired Chief Justice of Ontario, Sir William Mulock, on the platform. (The sponsoring Canadian Jewish Congress had invited Albert Einstein to speak but, unable to attend, he sent a gently reproving wire from Princeton, expressing the hope that Canada would open its sparcely populated land in the emergency.)[21] As usual in the thirties, the Jews' most sincere friends were sectors of organized labour and of the United Church, whose spokesmen urged the government to open its doors to the victims of Nazism. They were the exceptions; most of English Canada was ready to extend its sympathy to the refugees but not much else.

The cautious government of Mackenzie King would not even go that far. Adhering to a policy of non-interference in the internal affairs of another country, King would not commit himself to an official denunciation of the Nazi pogroms. The *Globe and Mail,* which had been editorializing on keeping Canada British ever since the *anschluss* raised the spectre of mass Jewish immigration, was nev-

---

*Despite the efforts of the 150 representative citizens and representatives of 40 organizations, who composed the Committee, the public response was poor. Kirkconnell, *Twilight of Liberty,* p. 61.

ertheless strongly critical of "Canada's Silent Voice," as it head-lined a November 18 editorial:

> The shock given the civilized world by the latest demonstration of Nazi barbarity made not a dent in the complacency of Can-ada's government so far as the country can see. Prime Minister King has taken refuge upon occasion in the thought that there is a time and place for all things. He has not found time and place to say what he could have said truthfully and vigorously: that Canadians will never forgive or attempt to understand the moral degeneration which leads a nation's majority to prey in hatefulness upon a minority.

While King said nothing, the Conservative opposition came out openly against Jewish immigration. Speaking in Quebec, the new leader, Robert Manion, opposed the entry of refugees on the grounds of the current unemployment. Nor were the average politi-cians of the two major parties any more in favour of an open-door policy than their leaders. A poll of Ontario federal and provincial members showed a consensus of agreement with Manion. Only the CCF took the humanitarian view and called for admission of a fair quota of refugees .

As for the civil service, if Chester Walters, Ontario's Deputy Minister of the Treasury Department, was representative of its thinking, the refugees had no friends among officialdom. Addressing a Toronto audience in December, 1938, Walters suddenly changed his topic from municipal finance to immigration:

> We are losing our pride in the fact that we are British, and, worse than that, we are admitting into our family and we are conferring British citizenship upon those who are unworthy. We will rue the day that we have taken into our midst some of these outcasts of other nations . . . . Admitted into our house and given full citizenship, they become a festering sore. Admit-ted in any great numbers, they will surely destroy the fine civi-lization which we have received from our fathers.

The most influential man in government, however, was O.D. Skelton, Under-Secretary of State for External Affairs. Described by a *Globe and Mail* reporter as "the man behind the scenes on all international affairs including immigration of refugees," he was undoubtedly instrumental in retaining Canada's restrictive immigration laws in the face of what the same reporter called "the greatest pressure of any issue in recent years." Applications for immigration, mainly from professional people, were pouring into Canada, and the Jewish Liberal M.P.'s were pleading with the prime minister to adopt a humanitarian policy. Nevertheless, Canada stood firm, and in doing so was little different from the other democratic nations. The Chamberlain government announced that Great Britain would admit refugee children on a temporary basis but would not allow mass Jewish immigration because of unemployment and "a deep-rooted opposition to alien immigration." Nevertheless, the United Kingdom did provide a home for about 65,000 of the refugees.[22] Of more dire consequence was Britain's decision in 1939, as the mandatory power in Palestine, to severely restrict Jewish immigration.[23] In the United States the immigration quotas remained unchanged. Roosevelt did what he could by extending visitors' permits but, as with the war itself, he could not move too far beyond public opinion. In the end, Canada admitted about eight thousand refugees, about the same number as Australia. Testifying before a Senate Committee in 1946, the research director of the Canadian Jewish Congress provided documented proof that there had actually been additional constraints on Jewish immigrants in those years that did not apply to other groups.[24] The reluctance of the Canadian government to admit Jewish refugees in any great numbers was a fair reflection of public opinion, English as well as French. While unemployment was the reason cited for Canada's closed door, underlying it was a strong Anglo-Saxon nativism permeated with anti-semitism.

The clearest expression of Anglo-Saxon nativism came from the Canadian Corps Association. Shortly after the November pogrom, the veterans' organization sent a resolution to the prime minister, opposing any weakening of the immigration laws which could "tend to make Canada the dumping ground of Europe." Legislation should ensure that "future citizenship be predominantly British" and anyone else admitted should be of a racial origin permitting rapid and complete assimilation. They asked for an end to "special permit abuses" and indiscriminate European immigration:

Now is no time to bring in people who have nothing in common with us, who do not want to work in the open and who have no desire to come here other than to find a new home . . . . While viewing forced mass immigration [*sic*] as iniquitous, and with sincere sympathy for such distressed immigrants, the ex-servicemen believe that the best interests of all concerned will not be served by directing migration to areas in which unemployment is predominant, where climatic conditions are unsuitable and under conditions where racial origin of the immigrants is such that complete assimilation is a foredoomed failure.[25]

The Corps' resolution suggested that the Jews be sent to Africa.

Undoubtedly encouraged by the veterans' stand, Arcand and Farr, who had been lying low in Ontario because of the prevalent anti-Nazi feeling, resurfaced and announced a three-month drive to protest against any Jewish immigration. The campaign began on December 5 in Toronto with a meeting attended by a hundred and fifty supporters and twenty-five Blueshirts. Arcand was the main speaker and after introducing a plan to get every Gentile storekeeper to display a sticker in his window proclaiming his religion, he proceeded to discuss a local matter of interest—the sudden resignation, just as suddenly rescinded, of the Toronto Chief of Police, Brigadier-General Draper. Arcand's version was that the Reds had tried to oust Chief Draper because he was their most bitter opponent, and he eulogized the chief for his service to the community. A clever tactician, Arcand probably hoped to remove some of the stigma attached to his party by associating himself with the forces of law and order. It is doubtful if Draper appreciated this gratuitous support.

The fascists' campaign petered out almost immediately. Actually Farr's Ontario Nationalist Party had never taken hold. After the national convention he had tried to keep up the momentum, ostentatiously holding uniformed drills in downtown Toronto halls and issuing provocative statements from time to time. But the only new recruits he managed to attract were a small number of teenage boys. By the winter, most of the veterans and militia had deserted his legions and the Italian members were reported to be defecting to the Canadian Union of Fascists. Moreover, strong-arm tactics at a meeting in North York, where Blueshirts punched and kicked a man in the audience, created very bad publicity. Basically, however, fascism in Ontario in the year leading up to the war was dead because it had no issues to appeal to. It could not appeal to isolationist sentiment as in Quebec, nor was the large German population as susceptible to Nazi propaganda as that of the West. Only its stand on Jewish immigration was apt to stir a popular response, but even those who agreed with the fascists, such as the Canadian Corps, were too anti-fascist to have anything to do with them.

Internment

In the year that was to see Canada once more at war with Germany, feeling against the Nazis was running high. A typical incident occurred in Calgary in the spring when a group of veterans threatened to forceably break up a scheduled Bund meeting. In fact the year began with an uproar over a pro-Hitler radio broadcast by a German consular official in Montreal. The *Toronto Star* called it "the most blatant and offensive Nazi propaganda yet unloosed," and the Canadian Corps Association demanded a thorough investigation and deportation of the speaker.[1] While the CBC was reviewing the case of "the Heil Hitler broadcast" (as the press dubbed it), a series of articles appeared in the *Winnipeg Tribune* exposing a direct connection between German government officials and Nazi propaganda in Manitoba. Scanning some records in the Provincial Secretary's office, a reporter had discovered that the major shareholders of the Bundist paper, the *Deutsche Zeitung,* were a former German consul, an official of the North German Lloyd Steamship Line and an agent for the Leipzig Fair. Moreover, the *Tribune* printed a translation of a *Zeitung* article attacking British Imperialism.[2] The *Winnipeg Free Press* followed up the *Tribune's* revelations with stories of Nazism among local Germans. It quoted authoritative sources as saying that literature was pouring into the Mennonite towns from Canadian fascist headquarters in Montreal.[3]

In the House of Commons the CCF finally forced the government to take a stand on Nazi propaganda. On January 19 M.J. Coldwell declared:

Here and in other legislatures of this Dominion we hear of the need to keep communist propaganda out of the country but so far no attempt has been made to keep out vicious Nazi propaganda which is attacking a minority in this country.

A few days later the CCF party leader, J.S. Woodsworth, asked the government what action it planned to take with regard to the exposures in the Winnipeg press. Apparently sensing that public reaction was too strong for more temporizing, King promised to report to the House very soon on the RCMP inquiry then in progress, and went so far as to point an accusing finger at the German consuls for their propaganda work. It was the first official admission that subversive activity was regarded seriously in Ottawa.

It might have been supposed that, in the anti-Nazi temper of the times, anti-semitism would decline. But this was not so. Far from receding, it was actually growing. Much of this was due to the work of Arcand, Farr and other Canadian Nazis. Commenting in 1939 on "the amazing growth of anti-semitism" during the past five years, the Canadian Jewish Congress attributed it to a transition from unorganized activity to

> activity sponsored by national organizations, directed by professional agents. It is this professional aspect of anti-semitism which has given an entirely new status to anti-Jewish functions, has aroused unprecedented anti-Jewish feeling, and has brought the Jewish community face to face with a situation somewhat similar to that existing in Germany in the early years of the Nazi movement.[4]

Undoubtedly the fascists had crystallized the incoherent anti-Jewish feeling. But the immediate cause of an intensified anti-semitism was the pressure to allow in Jewish refugees.

The government's decision to do nothing about the refugees was first indicated in a speech by the Secretary of State, Fernand Rinfret. Speaking in Montreal in January 1939, he announced: "Despite all sentiments of humanity, so long as Canada has an unemployment problem there will be no 'open door' for political refugees here." King and Lapointe initially denied that this was official policy, but a few days later when parliament reconvened, the Throne Speech preserved an eloquent silence on the refugee question. Despite A.A. Heaps' efforts to convince the House that there was a difference between immigration and asylum for victims of persecution, neither the government nor the opposition could be moved to offer any help to the refugees. It was at this point too that Wilfrid LaCroix, a Liberal member from Quebec, introduced the St. Jean-Baptiste Society petition, with its tens of thousands of signatures, opposing any admission of Jewish immigrants.

A few voices of dissent were heard. Surprisingly, one came from the former leader of the Conservatives, R.B. Bennett, who, in spite of his party's stand, spoke out for selective immigration of refugees. "There is an obligation upon this Christian country," he declared, "to do its share towards the relief of misery and suffering." Fine words, yet of little force and no cost to the speaker because this was Bennett's farewell address before departing to take up residence in England.

The National Committee on Refugees, representing "small-1" liberal opinion, pressed vigorously for providing asylum but, notwithstanding some impressive names on its letterhead, had little influence either on the government or on the general public. Probably more influential was Judith Robinson, an outspoken champion of civil liberties who wrote a regular column for the *Globe and Mail.* In a slashing attack on the Canadian leaders for their lack of humanity, she charged King, Lapointe and Manion with toadying to sectional prejudices and reminded them of Jesus's reprimand: "I was a stranger and ye took me not in." Turning to the petition of the St. Jean-Baptiste Society, she pictured John the Baptist himself being hustled out of the country because the petition in his name insisted that immigration laws should not be relaxed for Semites under any circumstances. Departing from the conventional wisdom of the thirties, which held that immigration should cease in a time of unemployment, she propounded the view, just then becoming current, that people make work as well as perform it, since the worker is also a consumer. In the mordant style that was her hallmark Robinson castigated her fellow Canadians:

> The idea that eleven million short-sighted natives will be left in peace forever to spread themselves, their natural increase and their unsolved unemployment problem over an undeveloped half-continent may be restful for Mr. Rinfret, but it doesn't make sense in the year Hitler 1939.[5]

The fullest condemnation of Canadian policy came from the Reverend Claris Silcox in March 1939, a few days after Germany swallowed up the entire state of Czechoslovakia. Silcox was a recognized authority on Christian-Jewish relations, having written several books on the subject. More of a social worker than a minister, he was general secretary of the Christian Social Council of Canada and from that vantage point was one of the authentic voices of the Canadian conscience. Speaking in Convocation Hall at the University of Toronto, Silcox analysed Canadian indifference to the plight of the European Jews. "There are half a dozen major reasons for our unwillingness to seize the opportunity to enrich our Canadian life with some of the cream of Europe's sometime citizenry," he told his comfortable, upper middle-class audience. In the first place, there was the "intellectual and moral confusion of our people," which he attributed largely to the lack of outstanding leadership. Secondly, there was the problem of the Canadian unemployed; but, he said, few people realized that what Canada needed was new industries to develop its raw materials and people to be both the producers and consumers for these new industries. Thirdly, there was the opposition from the farming sector to settling more people on the land and thus increasing the glut of farm products. Silcox concurred that mechanization had rendered much of the present agricultural population superfluous, and he criticized the government for its "incredibly unrealistic" policy of giving preference to agricultural applicants. (The dictum that farmers were the only desirable immigrants was continually invoked to disqualify the Jewish refugees and led to some contrived newspaper pictures planted by their well-wishers, showing urban types wearing bandanas and holding spades and hoes.) Fourthly, Silcox stated bluntly, there was "the fear of certain industrialists and businessmen concerning what may happen to them if energetic, shrewd refugees were permitted to enter and initiate some competitive industries, or general businesses; especially—may I blurt it out—if they are Jews." For his fifth reason Silcox named "the suspicion cultivated in French Canada of all immigration." His sixth reason was the spread of Nazi propaganda, particularly in Quebec, Ontario, Manitoba and Saskatchewan where Nazis had been most active.

To conclude his "Post-Mortem on Refugees," Mr. Silcox came to "perhaps the all-important reason . . . the existence throughout

Canada, but in some centres more manifest than in others, of a latent anti-semitism." He told his audience, "I would if I had time present you with a list of almost unbelievable and malicious falsehoods circulated against the Jews right in our own city. One is kept busy running these lies to the ground . . . "[6]

Certainly anti-semitic propaganda was flowing freely in Toronto in 1939. The British-Israel Federation was selling copies of the Protocols of Zion, while a wealthy property owner, whose chauffeur was seen with a swastika on his uniform, indulged his fanatical anti-semitism by mailing pamphlets to government and business acquaintances and by addressing church youth groups on the alleged "Jewish menace." Masses of the vicious pamphlet, "The Key to the Mystery," were still being distributed in the city by John Ross Taylor and in a number of other Ontario towns by local fascist groups. Since Mussolini had signed the Pact of Steel with Hitler, most of the Italo-Canadian press had become intensely pro-Nazi and anti-semitic, and it was said on good authority that some Canadian fascist publications were printed in the plant of an Italian fascist newspaper in Toronto.[7]

Meanwhile, little was heard of Farr, although he was known to be drilling his Blueshirt squads. Arcand had invested him with the title of National Organizer and from his headquarters on Pearl Street in Toronto, Farr despatched membership forms and propaganda material. One of his recipients was William Crane, a forty-year-old unemployed tailor in Halifax who was trying to organize a fascist party in Nova Scotia.[8] Crane had apparently approached Arcand in the spring of 1939 to accept his little group into the National Unity Party, and Arcand, who still harboured national hopes, accepted this tiny windfall graciously:

> The tenor of your propaganda is exactly the one we have carried on in this province for the last ten years, and in Ontario and the Western Provinces since 1933. Gradually, all Canadians thinking alike are uniting for defence of our civilization and reclaiming of our heritage from Jews' clutches. I am convinced your group and particularly yourself will be welcomed with great pleasure by Headquarters.[9]

All through the summer Arcand sent words of encouragement

to his new lieutenant in Nova Scotia. In July he despatched an autographed photo via Daniel O'Keefe, the party's New Brunswick
organizer. It appears that Crane was not making much headway,
for the same month Arcand professed himself "glad to hear of your
progress though slow."[10] He sought to impress Crane with personal
references to Mosley, who still sent him leaflets and exchanged lau-
datory cables with him. He advised Crane to build his movement
on the masses and not to wait for the bourgeoisie to awaken—"as in
Spain, it may never do so."[11] In the summer they met face to face
and afterwards Arcand flattered: "I am convinced you are the type
to carry through in your province."[12]

While fascism was almost dead in the rest of the country, in
Quebec Arcand and his friends were still thriving. A case in point
was Jean Tissot, the fascist policeman who, after losing his job as
Rouyn's chief of police, was appointed an inspector for the Quebec
Liquor Commission and, in 1939, placed in charge of revolver permits for the district of Montreal.[13] It was undoubtedly an exaggera-
tion to say, as the anti-fascist editor of *L'Autorité* did in August
1939, that "a fascist wave is unfurling on the province," but certainly Arcand was far from a spent force. His National Unity Party
meetings, mainly in Italian church halls, were attracting large
crowds. He even timed a public rally in Quebec City to coincide
with the royal visit. The fact that the Blueshirts on duty and many
of the large audience of five to six hundred were strangers, para-
chuted in for the occasion, indicates that Arcand had staged the
event in the hope of capitalizing on anti-monarchical sentiment.
But the provincial capital gave an exuberant welcome to the King
and Queen, and Arcand's performance elicited protests from the
Quebec Labour Council and other groups, as well as outraged letters to the Minister of Justice from individual French Canadians.[14]
That Arcand was beginning to alarm the provincial authorities is
clear from the fact that, at this time, the Quebec Provincial Police
set up a special department, under a nephew of the Lieutenant-
Governor, to investigate fascism and Nazism in the province.

That summer found Arcand occupied with an anti-semitic
campaign in the resort area of the Laurentians, just north of Montreal. It was fertile ground for him. Every summer the little French
villages beside the mountain lakes became swollen with visitors,
many of whom were Jewish—as high as 35 to 40 percent in a place

like Ste. Agathe. As often happens, the townsfolk resented the summer visitors and since, in this case, so many of the vacationers were Jewish, there had been some anti-semitic incidents. By 1939 there were a large number of Jewish-owned camps, hotels and cottages, and local resentment had risen accordingly. The situation was ripe for Arcand. His Laurentian offensive began in the village of St. Faustin. Addressing an audience of two thousand after Sunday Mass on July 23, he whipped up their resentment against their Jewish neighbours. Immediately afterwards, anti-Jewish signs were posted both in St. Faustin and in the neighbouring village of Ste. Agathe, and vandals attacked a hotel owned by a Jewish widow. Matters came to a head the following Sunday when one Canon Charland adjured the parishioners of Ste. Agathe to neither rent nor sell their property to Jews. After his sermon at least two hundred posters appeared as if by magic in the village. Printed in both languages, the English version read: "Jews not wanted in Sainte-Agathe so scram while the going is good." These events attracted a good deal of publicity. *Le Canada* reported that the canon was supported by the curé of Ste. Agathe, who had announced that he was forming a committee to decide who could buy land in the village and its environs. The *Montreal Gazette* gave full coverage to the story, uncovering new incidents every day: there was an attempt to burn the bridge to a Jewish hotel; an eleven-year-old boy, driving a milk truck, struck a Jewish woman with his whip; a hotel in Ste. Agathe placed a sign on the reception desk stating: "This hotel has a reciprocal agreement with two Jewish hotels whereby we recommend them to prospective Jewish guests, and they, in turn, recommend our hotel to Christians."[15]

Just how much of a role Arcand played in these events is open to conjecture. It is highly significant that a steady stream of anti-semitic propaganda arrived from Montreal to fuel the fires. For example, all non-Jews in Ste. Agathe received a circular in the mail entitled "On Guard." In part it read: "Wake up before it is too late. Is our town French Canadian? Is it to be a rendezvous of Jews? The problem is much more serious than we think." Despite the attempt to make it appear a local effort, the mailing address was Montreal. Directly attributable to Arcand was a large-scale distribution of *Le Combat National,* the successor to his *Le Fasciste Canadien.* Arcand himself took a proprietary pride in the whole affair, writing to William Crane in Halifax of "the great awakening in the Laurentian Mountains here."[16]

In his home province Arcand made no attempt to conceal his fascism. In his speeches he attacked democracy and praised dictatorship. Even after the Danzig crisis and the German-Russian Pact in August 1939, *L'Illustration Nouvelle* (now generally referred to as the "fascist paper") called for a four-power pact and absolved Hitler from responsibility for the breakdown of world peace. According to Arcand, Danzig was a German city and Poland, Great Britain and France had no right to defend it against Hitler. He charged that all democracies had war parties, supported by financial magnates and international news agencies, and he claimed that Poland, not Germany, wanted war. He painted a picture of Germany encircled and (still under the injunction to stay clear of overt anti-semitism in the tabloid) cryptically accused the 'Freemasons' of masterminding the democracies' resistance to Herr Hitler. In contrast, the rest of the Quebec press held Hitler to blame for the world crisis (at the same time expressing reservations editorially regarding Canada's part in the coming struggle). As Florent Lefebvre expressed it in his pamphlet, "The French-Canadian Press and the War," *L'Illustration Nouvelle* continued to exhibit "a strange benevolence towards the Third Reich and a systematic slander of democracies." Writing in 1940, Lefebvre went on to say that, so biased was Arcand in favour of Germany, that there were rumours in editorial offices in August 1939 that the tabloid's policy was of "foreign inspiration".[17]

On September 10, 1939, Canada declared war. One of the minor consequences was that Arcand was ordered to cease from holding public meetings and to disband the National Unity Party. His compliance was superficial only; the organization simply went underground. A hidden printing press on St. Lawrence Boulevard churned out anonymous pamphlets such as "The Jews and The War," and Madame Arcand and Lionel St. Jean (alias Papineau), an employee of *La Presse* and long-time Arcand aide, conducted small meetings in private homes. According to the author of the *Standard* article, Arcand continued to recruit even after he was told to disband. The legionnaires became a veritable army in miniature, with companies, patrols and sergeant-majors who served as recruiting officers. (The same source claimed that Arcand and his follow-ers wanted a German victory because they believed it would bring them to power.) Arcand even managed to circumvent the ban on public meetings by operating behind the front of a sympathetic priest called Father Fabien. On one occasion, in March 1940, over six hundred people met in a church hall on Pius IX Boulevard, os-tensibly to hear an address by Father Fabien. They were, in fact, attending a meeting of the National Unity Party.[18]

Although not so boldly, NUP branches in other cities were also functioning after the outbreak of war. In Ontario Farr held small weekly meetings of about twenty faithful. The Regina branch dis-tributed a piece of anti-semitic propaganda entitled "An Open Let-ter to Gentile Businessmen," while in the Maritimes the NUP had four separate anti-semitic pamphlets in circulation.

But the fascist movement's days were numbered. The Nazi offensive in the spring turned the "phony" war into a reality. Den-mark and Norway collapsed before the German advance, and in May Hitler invaded the Netherlands, Belgium and northern France. In Canada there was great popular indignation about the Quislings and other subversive elements that had facilitated the Nazi conquests. With the first Canadian boys going overseas, war hysteria was mounting rapidly. From organizations, from municipal and even provincial governments, demands went forth to Ottawa to intern all enemy aliens and Nazi sympathizers. The press was full of talk about a "fifth column" in this country. Veterans' associa-tions could hardly be contained from forming vigilante committees to take the law into their own hands.

The news that Mosley and his aides had been arrested in Eng-land triggered government action. In Montreal, RCMP and local po-lice raided Arcand's headquarters and a number of private homes of suspected fascists. They seized truckloads of swastika banners, maps, membership lists, and anti-semitic propaganda postmarked Germany. This was followed a few days later by a round-up of the fascists themselves. Arcand (to quote the *Toronto Star*) was "captured in his hide-out in the Quebec mountains." Taken with him was his current chief lieutenant, a dentist named Dr. Noel Lecarie, who was discovered to have over $7,000 stuffed in his pockets. Six others were arrested in Montreal, one in Ottawa, and two in Toronto.

In less than three weeks the eleven fascists were brought to trial in a Montreal court.* RCMP Inspector Clifford Harvison, the officer in charge of the round-up, produced a seized document purported to be a plan for a fascist army of seventy thousand. Also exhibited were dozens of letters to Arcand from Nazis and international fascists which provided strong circumstancial evidence of his affiliation with these groups. Proceeding under the wartime Defence of Canada Regulations, events moved swiftly. Two days after the preliminary inquiry, the Minister of Justice, Ernest Lapointe, announced that the fascists had been interned. He stated that he had seen the exhibits at the trial and since they clearly showed "communication and intelligence with enemies," he had ordered the internment. At the same time the National Unity Party (along with other fascist and communist organizations) was declared illegal.

The fascist movement in Canada was suppressed, not out of any moral repugnance, but because Germany had become the enemy. The public outcry which led to government action makes this very clear. Known to be distributing Nazi propaganda and suspected of dealings with the Nazis, Arcand and his associates were regarded as potential Quislings and thus a threat to the national security.

The fascists were interned at Fredericton, New Brunswick. Major Scott died in internment and several lesser figures were released before the end of the war, but Arcand and his chief aides remained in the camp until July 1945. On their release they launched a three and a half million dollar damages suit against the federal government, which was dismissed by the Exchequer Court. The public quickly forgot them. In 1949 Arcand attempted a comeback by running unsuccessfully for parliament. In his poverty and obscurity he was helped out by his old friend, Premier Duplessis, who provided him with translating and editing assignments.[19] Until his death in 1967 Arcand continued his anti-semitic propaganda,

---

*At the preliminary hearing Salluste Lavery, who was acting for several of the defendants, created a scene by shouting out that Arcand and his lieutenants were "the greatest Canadians in Canada." He added characteristically that the Jews were responsible for the war. (*Montreal Star*, June 5, 1940).

but defamation of a race was unacceptable in the two decades after Auschwitz.

During the thirties Canadian fascists had been permitted, in the name of freedom of speech, to spread their message of hate unhindered, but post-war revulsion over Hitler's enormities led to legislation to combat overt racism. Fascist movements and racism did not vanish, but withdrew to await a more welcoming climate.

Notes and References

INTRODUCTION

1. E.J. Garland, "The Lost Best West," *Addresses Delivered Before the Canadian Club of Toronto, Season 1930-31* (Toronto, 1931), p.225.
2. W.A. Gordon, Minister of Labour and Immigration, quoted in *Labour Gazette* (December 1932), p.1304.
3. L.W. Moffit, *Maclean's* (April 1, 1931), 14.
4. H. Arendt, *The Origins of Totalitarianism* (2nd. ed.: 1967), p.158.

CHAPTER I

1. "Arcand, Adrien," in *Biographies Canadiennes-Françaises* (Montreal, 1931), p.495.
2. *Le Goglu,* January 31, 1930.
3. Public Archives of Canada (P.A.C.), Bennett Papers, vol.653, Adrien Arcand to Bennett, memo dated April 8, 1930.
4. *Le Goglu,* October 17, 1930.
5. *Ibid.,* September 19, 1929.
6. *Ibid.,* November 29, 1929.
7. C.M. Bayley, "The Social Structure of the Italian and Ukrainian Immigrant Communities, Montreal, 1935-37," M.A. thesis unpublished, McGill University, 1939, p.180 *et seq.*
8. See J. Eayrs, "A Low Dishonest Decade: Aspects of Canadian External Policy, 1931-39," in H. Keenleyside *et al., The Growth of Canadian Policies in External Affairs* (North Carolina, 1960), p.69.
9. *Le Goglu*, March 21, 1930.
10. *Canadian Annual Review of Public Affairs 1930-31,* (Toronto, 1931), pp.156, 158.
11. *Le Goglu,* March 28, 1930.
12. *Ibid.,* April 25, 1930.

13. P.A.C., Bennett Papers, vol.484, A.W. Reid to Bennett, December 27, 1929. (Arcand's subsidy from the Conservative party was first pointed out in M. La Terreur, *Les Tribulations des Conservateurs au Québec de Bennett à Diefenbaker* (Quebec, 1973) p.16).
14. *Ibid.,* vol.653, Arcand to Bennett, memo dated dated January 14, 1931.
15. *Ibid.,* vol.484, A.D. Morgan to Bennett, May 26, 1930.
16. *Le Goglu,* May 16, 1930.
17. P.A.C., Bennett Papers, vol.484, Arcand to Bennett, May 22, 1930.
18. *Ibid.,* vol.653, Statement accompanying memo from Arcand to Bennett, dated January 14, 1931.
19. *Ibid.,* vol.653, Arcand and Joseph Ménard to Bennett, January 2, 1932.
20. *Ibid.,* vol.653, P.E. Blondin to Arthur Merriam, August 8, 1932.
21. *Ibid.,* vol.990, A.W. Reid to Bennett, May 14, 1936.
22. A. Arcand, "Chrétien ou Juif." Address delivered at the Monument National, November 3, 1930.
23. F. Edwards, "Fascism in Canada," part 1, *Maclean's* (April 15, 1938), 10.
24. *Le Devoir,* July 15, 1932.
25. P.A.C., Lapointe Papers, vol.22, R.J. Letourneau to Mackenzie King, February 14, 1938.
26. B. Figler, *Sam Jacobs, Member of Parliament* (Quebec, 1959), pp.26-27.
27. *Canadian Annual Review 1932* (Toronto, 1933), p.174; *Le Devoir,* January 28, 1932; *La Presse,* January 28, 1932.
28. *Le Devoir,* January 29, 1932.
29. *Ibid.,* February 1, 1932.
30. Quoted in *Le Devoir,* February 3, 1932.
31. *Le Miroir,* January 31, 1932.
32. *Le Devoir,* February 4, 1932; *ibid.,* February 9, 1932.
33. *Ibid.,* February 13, 1932.
34. Quoted in *Le Devoir,* February 6, 1932.
35. *La Presse,* February 16, 1932.
36. *Le Devoir,* February 17, 1932.
37. *Ibid.,* February 19, 1932.
38. *Le Goglu,* February 19, 19!32.

CHAPTER II

1. *Le Miroir,* March 13, 1932.
2. See Norman Cohn, "The Myth of the Jewish World-Conspiracy," *Commentary* (June, 1966), 35-42.
3. *Toronto Daily Star,* February 10, 1938.
4. E.C. Hughes, *French Canada in Transition* (Toronto, 1943), p.217.
5. Like Hitler in *Mein Kampf,* Arcand explicitly announced his plan of attack. See *Le Goglu,* March 3, 1933.
6. P.A.C., Bennett Papers, vol.653, Arcand to Bennett, June 4, 1932.

7. *Ibid.*, vol.653, Leslie Bell to Bennett, June 7, 1932.

8. *Ibid.*, vol.653, John A. Sullivan to Bennett, June 7, 1932.

9. *Ibid.*, vol.653, Armand Lavergne to Bennett, June 10, 1932.

10. *Le Fasciste Canadien,* November 1936.

11. P.A.C., Bennett Papers, vol.475, P.E. Blondin to Bennett, [March 1934].

12. *Le Devoir,* July 14, 15, 16, 1932.

13. *Ibid.,* September 13, 1932.

14. *Ibid.,* September 14, 1932.

15. *Ibid.,* February 11, 1933.

16. *Le Goglu,* March 3, 1933.

17. K.G.W. Ludecke, *I Knew Hitler* (New York, 1937), p. 541.

18. D.Martin, "Adrien Arcand, Fascist—An Interview," *The Nation* (February 26, 1938), 243.

19. Canadian Jewish Congress Archives (C.J.C.), K. Ludecke to Major Frank Pease, December 12, 1932. Copy. Many documents pertaining to the fascist movement were turned over to Congress by sympathizers or defectors.

20. Quoted in *Toronto Star,* June 19, 1940.

21. *Le Goglu,* February 10, 1933.

22. Address delivered by Joseph Ménard, October 20, 1933, at Palestre National, printed in *Le Patriote,* October 26, 1933.

23. *Le Patriote,* June 22, 1933.

24. P.A.C., Bennett Papers, vol.475, P.E. Blondin to Bennett, [March 1934].

25. *Le Devoir,* April 12, 1933.

26. *Le Goglu,* March 10, 1933.

CHAPTER III

1. M. Wade, *The French Canadians 1760-1967* (Rev.ed.; Toronto, 1968), II, 867.

2. *L'Action Nationale,* II (October, 1933), 152.

3. Printed in *ibid.,* II (September, 1933), 152.

4. *Le Devoir,* April 7, 1933.

5. *Ibid.,* April 12, 1933.

6. *Le Patriote,* May 18, 1933.

7. T.D. Bouchard, *Mémoires* (Montreal, 1960), III, 95.

8. *Le Patriote,* August 31, 1933.

9. *Ibid.,* July 20, 1933.

10. Cited in Figler, *Jacobs,* p.203.

11. C.J.C., Arcand to Major F. Pease, September 28, 1932. Copy. Arcand acknowledged authorship of this letter in an interview. (D. Martin, *The Nation,* February 26, 1938, p.243.)

12. The text of Arcand's February 22nd speech was reprinted in full in *Le Patriote*, March 8 and 15, 1934.

13. P.A.C., Bennett Papers, vol.475, P.E. Blondin to Bennett, [March 1934].

14. *Ibid.*, vol.484, J.E. Laforce to Bennett, April 11, 1934.

15. *Le Patriote*, April 5, 1934.

16. C.J.C., Minutes of the Dominion Executive, June 21, 1934.

17. C.J.C., Minutes of the Anti-Defamation Committee (A.D.C.), April 22, 1934.

18. C.J.C., Minutes, Dominion Executive, May 3, 1934.

19. C.J.C., A.D.C. Minutes, February 21, March 25, 1934.

20. Cited in S.E. Rosenberg, *The Jewish Community in Canada*, I (Toronto, 1970), 225.

21. *Le Fasciste Canadien*, No.1., June 1935.

22. C.J.C., A.D.C. Minutes, April 8, 1934.

23. *Le Patriote*, October 11, 1934.

24. *Ibid.*, October 18, 1934.

25. P.A.C., King Papers, vol.233, H.M. Caiserman to King, August 25, 1937.

26. *Montreal Gazette*, October 9, 1935.

27. *Ottawa Journal*, March 21, 1935.

28. *Ottawa Citizen*, March 8, 1935.

29. *Le Patriote*, October 10, 1935.

30. *Le Fasciste Canadien*, Nos. 4,5, September, October , 1935.

31. *Ibid.*, No. 4, September, 1935.

32. Edwards, "Fascism in Canada," 66.

33. *Montreal Gazette*, October 9, 1935.

CHAPTER IV

1. J.M. Gibbon, *Canadian Mosaic: The Making of a Northern Nation* (Toronto, 1938), p.77.

2. F.W. Baumgartner, "Central European Immigration," *Queen's Quarterly* (Winter, 1930), 183-92. The major prophet of the "decline of the Anglo-Saxon" was W.B. Hurd, professor of economics at Brandon College, Manitoba, and author of census monographs.

3. *Addresses Delivered Before the Canadian Club of Toronto, Season 1930-31* (Toronto, 1931), p.178.

4. *Globe and Mail*, July 13, 1937.

5. D.H. Wrong, "Ontario's Jews in the Larger Community" in A. Rose, ed., *A People and Its Faith*, (Toronto, 1959), p.53.

6. All statistical data on Jewish Canadians of the period is drawn from L. Rosenberg's *Canada's Jews: A Social and Economic Study of the Jews in Canada* (Montreal, 1939).

7. *Toronto Star*, August 26, 1933.

8. *Ibid.,* April 24, 1933.
9. E. Einbinder, "Study of Attitudes towards Jews in Toronto," M.A. thesis unpublished, University of Toronto, 1934, p.23.
10. C.E. Silcox and G.M. Fisher, *Catholics, Jews and Protestants: A Study of Relationships in the United States and Canada* (New York, 1934), p.48.
11. *Canadian Annual Review 1932,* p.126.
12. Telephone interview with J.J. Glass, October 6, 1972.
13. *Toronto Star,* March 1, 1933.
14. Wrong, "Ontario's Jews," p.53.
15. *Toronto Star,* April 24, 1933.
16. Wrong, "Ontario's Jews," p.53.
17. *Winnipeg Free Press,* August 12, 1933.
18. *Toronto Star,* August 2, 1933.
19. *Ibid.,* August 9, 1933.
20. *Ibid.*
21. *Ibid.,* August 8, 1933.
22. *Ibid.,* August 11, 1933.
23. *Ibid.,* August 8, 1933.
24. *Ibid.,* August 11, 1933.
25. Mackay, for one, disowned Bert specifically because he agreed to give up the swastika emblem. (*Ibid.,* August 15, 1933).
26. *Ibid.,* August 14, 1933.
27. *Ibid.*
28. *Ibid.,* August 15, 1933.
29. *Ibid.*
30. *Ibid.,* August 17, 1933.
31. *Ibid.,* August 18, 22, 1933. Typical of those arrested was a twenty-one-year-old boy who had been out of work for four years and, according to his mother, hung around the park most of the time. (*Ibid.,* August 19, 1933).
32. *Ibid.,* August 19, 1933.
33. *Ibid.*

CHAPTER V

1. W. Murray, "Continental Europeans in Western Canada," *Queen's Quarterly* (Winter, 1931), 63.
2. Gibbon, *Canadian Mosaic,* p.304.
3. *Ibid.,* p.410.
4. *Winnipeg Free Press,* January 10, 1934.
5. E. Wangenheim, "The Ukrainians: A Case Study of the Third Force," in P. Russell, ed., *Nationalism in Canada* (Toronto, 1966), p.82.

6. Z.A.B. Zeman, *Nazi Propaganda* (London, 1964), pp.67-73. Kurt Ludecke, who had been a one-man propaganda bureau in America before Hitler's accession, fell into disgrace in 1933—a victim of Goebbel's malice.

7. E.g., *Globe and Mail*, November 6, 1937.

8. P.A.C., Jacobs Papers, vol.8, H. Strauss to W.B. Schwab, May 26, 1933. Copy.

9. *Winnipeg Free Press*, June 27, 1934.

10. P.A.C., Jacobs Papers, vol.8.

11. P.A.C., Department of National Defence Records, Box 2496, Mrs Davidson to the Minister of Defence, March 2, 1934.

12. *Winnipeg Free Press*, March 17, 1934. Letter to editor from D.J. Loeppky, Winkler, Manitoba; *ibid.*, August 4, 1934.

13. F.H. Epp, "An Analysis of Germanism and National Socialism in the Immigrant Newspaper of a Canadian Minority Group, the Mennonites, in the 1930s," Doctoral thesis unpublished, University of Minnesota, 1965, p.3.

14. Dr. Henry Oeklers in *Winnipeg Tribune*, March 1, 1938, cited in Gibbon, *Canadian Mosaic*, p.188.

15. E.g., letter to editor of *Winnipeg Free Press* from German Canadian living in Winnipeg for thirty-five years (August 4, 1934).

16. Ludecke, *I Knew Hitler*, p.561.

17. *Winnipeg Free Press*, March 8, 1934; *Globe and Mail*, March 4, 1938.

18. Epp, " . . . the Mennonites," p.312.

19. *Winnipeg Free Press*, June 6, 1934.

20. Epp, ". . . the Mennonites," p.152.

21. *Winnipeg Free Press*, February 13, 1934.

22. *Ibid.*, February 21, 1934.

23. *Ibid.*, February 22, 1934.

24. *Ibid.*, February 23, 1934.

25. *Ibid.*, September 23, 1933.

26. *Stat. Man.* 1934, c.23, now *R.S.M.* 1954, c.60, s.20.

27. *Winnipeg Free Press*, June 13, 1934.

28. R. Benewick, *A Study of British Fascism, Political Violence and Public Order* (London, 1969), p.169.

29. *Winnipeg Free Press*, July 9, 1934.

30. *Ibid.*, September 22, 1934.

31. *Ibid.*, September 7, 1934; C.J.C., Minute Book, Dominion Executive, March 15, 1934.

32. P.A.C., National Defence Records, Box 2496, Lt.Col. G.L. Jennings to Col. H.D. Crerar, August 7, 1936. The observations of the medical student were later relayed to the Department of National Defence.

33. *Winnipeg Tribune*, January 11, 1939.

34. J. Gray, *The Winter Years, The Depression on the Prairies* (Toronto, 1966), p. 185.

CHAPTER VI

1. *Winnipeg Free Press,* June 23, 1934.
2. *Ibid.*
3. *Ibid.,* July 13, 1934.
4. Benewick, *British Fascism,* p.154.
5. *Winnipeg Free Press,* July 13, 1934.
6. *The Thunderbolt,* August 20, 1937.
7. W. Kirkconnell, *Twilight of Liberty* (Toronto, 1941), p.89.
8. C.J.C., L. Nadler, Shaunavon, Sask., to H.M. Caiserman, June 18, 1934.
9. *The Thunderbolt,* November 1937; C.J.C., L. Rosenberg to S.D. Levine, July 11, 1934; C.J.C., R.M. Johnstone to Tom King, n.d., copy enclosed in letter from Nadler to Caiserman, June 18, 1934.
10. C.J.C., L. Rosenberg to S.M. Selchen, Winnipeg, August 27, 1934.
11. *Globe and Mail,* December 8, 1937. E.g., Dr. R. Muir Johnstone, "Crop Failure and the Middle West," *The Thunderbolt,* August 20, 1937.
12. C.J.C., Johnstone to King, *supra.*
13. H.J. Schultz, "Portrait of a Premier: William Aberhart," in R. Cook, ed., *Politics of Discontent* (Toronto, 1967), p. 18.
14. W.F. Elsey, Woodstock, Ontario, to Magistrate S.A. Jones, Brantford, Ontario, February 26, 1935. Reproduced in facsimile in F. Rose, *Fascism Over Canada* (1938), p.20. Although the Communist, Rose, is a dubious authority, the letter is undoubtedly genuine on the basis of internal evidence.
15. *Le Patriote,* May 11, 1933.
16. *Toronto Star,* March 14, 1933.
17. S.A. Jones, "Fascism," *Empire Club of Canada: Addresses Delivered to the Members during the Year 1933-34* (Toronto, 1934), pp.403-18.
18. W.F. Elsey to S.A. Jones, *supra.*
19. *The Thunderbolt,* July 20, 1937.
20. Bayley, "Social Structure of the Italian Immigrant Community," p.189.
21. Canada, *House of Commons Debates 1936,* I, 674.
22. Rose, *Fascism Over Canada,* p.18. Bayley also mentions that Arcand's paper, *L'Illustration Nouvelle,* employed an Italian reporter.
23. *Winnipeg Free Press,* June 7, 1934. As well as acting for the Nationalists arrested after the marketplace riot, this Marino De Lucia also represented Whittaker in the Tobias libel case. (Examination for Discovery, *Tobias v. Whittaker and Neuman,* December 28, 1934).

CHAPTER VII

1. P.A.C., Arcand Papers, vol.1, Arcand to Daniel Johnston, May 3, 1965.
2. C.J.C., Gilbert Larue to H.M. Caiserman, June 30, 1937.
3. P.A.C., Arcand Papers, vol.1., Arcand to Daniel Johnson, May 3, 1965.
4. C.J.C., Joint Public Relations Committee 1938, unsigned memo, August 2, 1938.
5. S., "Embryo Fascism in Quebec," *Foreign Affairs* (April, 1938), 455.
6. Harold Dingman in *Globe and Mail*, January 5, 1938.
7. André Laurendeau quoted in Wade, *French Canadians, II, 908-09.*
8. P.A.C., Woodsworth Papers, vol.5, E. Forsey to Ernest Lapointe, November 3, 1936.
9. *En Avant,* November 26, 1937; *Le Jour,* December 4, 1937.
10. P.A.C., Lapointe Papers, vol.22, R.J. Letourneau to Lapointe, November 29, 1937.
11. *Le Devoir,* February 4, 1937.
12. Edwards, "Fascism in Canada," 66; T.D. Bouchard in *En Avant,* December 3, 1937.
13. *En Avant,* December 3, 1937.
14. *Montreal Star,* December 15, 1937; P.A.C., Lapointe Papers, vol.22, Private secretary to Minister of Justice to Commissioner S.T. Wood, July 16, 1940.
15. Edwards, "Fascism in Canada," 66.
16. C.J.C., Dr. G. Lambert to H.M. Caiserman, September 27, 1937.
17. C.J.C., H.M. Caiserman to Oscar Cohen, October 12, 1937.
18. P.A.C., King Papers, vol.233, H.M. Caiserman to the Prime Minister, August 25, 1937.
19. P.A.C., Woodsworth Papers, vol.9. Copy of Lalanne pamphlet.
20. C.J.C., Minute Book, Central Division 1938, II, February 8, June 14, 1938.
21. *L'Action Paroissiale Notre-Dame-du-Perpetuel-Secours,* September 1937. Translation in letter from H.M. Caiserman to Rabbi J. Stern, October 15, 1937. (C.J.C., Joint Public Relations 1937, Miscellaneous correspondence.)
22. C.J.C., J.E.M. Hains to Cardinal Villeneuve, April 14, 1937. Copy.
23. C.J.C., H.M. Caiserman to M. Seigler, October 25, 1937.
24. *Globe and Mail,* February 2, 1938. Woodsworth raised this matter in the House of Commons.
25. C.J.C., Minute Book, Central Division 1937, II, H.M. Caiserman to Oscar Cohen, [August, 1937].
26. P.A.C., King Papers, vol. 23, memo initialled E.A.P[ickering] to the Prime Minister, September 10, 1937.
27. *Ibid.,* cabinet memo dated September 14, 1937.
28. *The Thunderbolt,* November 1937; Rose, *Fascism Over Canada,* p.21.

29. *Globe and Mail,* December 8, 1937.
30. E.S. McLeod, "Shadow Over Canada," *The Nation* (February 12, 1938), 177-78.
31. *Globe and Mail,* November 11, 1937.
32. McLeod, "Shadow Over Canada," 178.
33. *Globe and Mail,* December 8, 1937; *Montreal Star,* December 15, 1937.
34. *Toronto Star,* July 5, 1938.
35. Exhibit at trial of Arcand *et al,* quoted in *Toronto Star,* June 19, 1940.

CHAPTER VIII

1. *Globe and Mail,* June 2, 1937.
2. *Ibid.,* August 3, 1937.
3. *Ibid.,* September 8, 1937.
4. J. Eayrs, *In Defence of Canada: Appeasement and Rearmament* (Toronto, 1965), pp.46-47.
5. A.A. McLeod, National Secretary, League Against War and Fascism, quoted in *Globe and Mail,* August 5, 1937.
6. Eayrs, *In Defence of Canada,* p.51.
7. Quoted by Samuel Factor, M.P., during the House debate on renewing the Canadian-German trade agreement. (*House of Commons Debates* 1937, III, 2738).
8. J. Eayrs, "A Low Dishonest Decade: Aspects of Canadian External Policy, 1931-39," in H. Keenleyside *et al., The Growth of Canadian Policies in External Affairs* (North Carolina, 1960), p.70.
9. *Globe and Mail,* November 4, 1937.
10. *The Globe,* January 21, 1935.
11. *Globe and Mail,* November 15, 1937.
12. E.g., report of campaign speech in *Globe and Mail,* September 17, 1937.
13. *Ibid.,* August 5, 1937.
14. A copy of this handbill is in Toronto Municipal Archives.
15. *Globe and Mail,* November 8, 1937.
16. *Ibid.,* November 9, 1937.
17. Telephone interview with J.J. Glass, October 6, 1972.
18. *Globe and Mail,* November 26, 27, 30, December 1, 2, 3, 8, 1937.
19. *Ibid.,* December 2, 1937.
20. *Toronto Star,* February 10, 1938.
21. Edwards, "Fascism in Canada," 66.
22. D. Martin, "Adrien Arcand, Fascist—An Interview," *The Nation* (February 26, 1938), 243.
23. Edwards, "Fascism in Canada," 10.
24. *Globe and Mail,* January 5, 1938.
25. Martin, "Adrien Arcand, Fascist," 241.
26. *Toronto Star,* July 5, 1938.
27. Rose, *Fascism,* p.21.

28. Kirkconnell, *Twilight of Liberty,* p.90.
29. *Globe and Mail,* January 31, 1938.
30. *Ibid.,* February 8, 1938; *L'Illustration Nouvelle,* February 7, 1938.
31. *House of Commons Debates 1938,* I, 174.
32. *Globe and Mail,* February 5, 1938.
33. P.A.C., Lapointe Papers, vol. 22, Adrien Arcand to Lapointe, February 5, 1938.
34. *Toronto Star,* February 5, 1938.
35. *Globe and Mail,* February 23, 1938.
36. Edwards, "Fascism in Canada," 66.

CHAPTER IX

1. Edwards, "Fascism in Canada," part 2, *Maclean's* (May 1, 1938), 15.
2. *Globe and Mail,* June 4, 1938.
3. *Ibid.,* June 7, 1938.
4. *Ibid.,* January 5, 1938.
5. *Ibid.,* June 17, 1938.
6. Interview with A. Bartelotti, January 28, 1974.
7. *Globe and Mail,* May 3, 1938.
8. *Ibid.,* July 14, 21, 1938; Edwards, "Fascism in Canada," Parts 1 and 2.
9. *L'Autorité,* July 9, 1938.
10. *Ibid.*
11. *Globe and Mail,* May 20, 1938.
12. *La Presse,* May 20, 1938.
13. *Globe and Mail,* May 26, 1938.
14. *Ibid.,* May 28, 1938; P.A.C., National Defence Records, Box 2496, Lt.Col. Jennings, Director of Criminal Investigation, R.C.M.P., to Col. H.D. Crerar, Director of Military Operations and Intelligence, August 7, 1936.
15. *House of Commons Debates* 1938, IV, 4418.
16. *Globe and Mail,* June 6, 1938.
17. *Ibid.,* June 8, 1938.
18. *Toronto Star,* June 8, 1938.
19. *Globe and Mail,* July 15, 1938.
20. *Toronto Star,* July 4, 1938. In June 1938 the Native Sons of Canada (a veterans' organization which described itself as having a cross-relationship with the Canadian Corps [*Globe,* September 3, 1935]) officially denied "prevalent" reports in Montreal that it was linked with or supported fascism. Its national president assured the Minister of Justice that "the organization would not permit any member to take part in a movement of this nature." (P.A.C., Lapointe Papers, vol.22, R.W. Carr to Lapointe, June 14, 1938.) This denial overlooks the fact that Salluste Lavery and Dr. P.E. Lalanne were active members of both the Native Sons and Arcand's fascist movement.

21. P.A.C., Lapointe Papers, vol.22, T.C. Davis to Lapointe, March 29, 1938.

22. "I Belonged to Arcand's Party," *Montreal Standard Magazine,* June 8, 1940.

CHAPTER X

1. C.J.C., L. Rosenberg to G. Dealtry, Trades and Labour Congress, Saskatoon, July 26, 1938.

2. Epp, " . . . National Socialism in the Immigrant Newspaper of a Canadian Minority Group, the Mennonites," p.186.

3. H. Fries, letter to editor of *Regina Leader-Post,* May 4, 1938. Fries contributed the occasional article to *The Thunderbolt* (e.g. August 20, 1937).

4. *Saskatoon Star-Phoenix,* May 5, 1938.

5. *House of Commons Debates* 1938, III, 3197.

6. P.A.C., Lapointe Papers, vol.22.

7. Cited in P.R. Sinclair, "The Saskatchewan C.C.F. and the Communist Party in the 1930s," *Saskatchewan History* (Winter, 1973), 9.

8. *House of Commons Debates* 1940, I, 238.

9. C.J.C., W. Keller to H.M. Caiserman, March 22, 1938.

10. P.A.C., National Defence Records, Box 2497, anonymous sender, April 18, 1938.

11. P.A.C., Lapointe Papers, vol.22, Secretary, Canadian Corps Association to Lapointe, April 28, 1939.

12. C.J.C., M. Seigler to H.M. Caiserman, October 12, 1938.

13. Wade, *French Canadians,* II, 917.

14. C.J.C., W. Schirmer to D. O'Leary, undated reply to a letter from O'Leary, April 2, 1939. Unknown to his correspondent, Mr. O'Leary was a journalist planning to write an article on Nazi activity in Canada.

15. "I Belonged to Arcand's Party," *Montreal Standard Magazine,* June 8, 1940.

16. *L'Illustration Nouvelle,* September 21, 1938.

17. J. Hoare, "Swastika Over Quebec," *Saturday Night* (September 9, 1939), 3.

18. C.J.C., memo with name of sender blacked out, October 5, 1938.

19. P.A.C., Lapointe Papers, vol.22, "206" to L.P. Picard, private secretary to the Minister of Justice, August 22, 1939. For a full discussion of Bouchard's "lengthy flirtation" with Social Credit, see M. Oliver, "The Social and Political Ideas of French-Canadian Nationalists, 1920-45," unpublished Ph.D. dissertation, McGill University, 1956.

20. C.J.C., H.M. Caiserman to Cardinal Villeneuve, August 30, 1938.

21. *Globe and Mail,* November 21, 1938.

22. A. Sharf, *The British Press and Jews Under Nazi Rule* (London, 1964), p.155.

23. *Ibid.*, p.182.
24. *Canada, Senate, Proceedings of the Standing Committee on Immigration and Labour* (Ottawa, 1946), pp.172-74. Evidence of Louis Rosenberg, Research Director, C.J.C.
25. *Globe and Mail,* November 19, 1938.

CHAPTER XI

1. *Toronto Star,* January 4, 1939.
2. *Winnipeg Tribune,* January 11, 17, 1939.
3. *Winnipeg Free Press,* January 27, 1939.
4. C.J.C., Report of Executive Secretary, Central Division [Oscar Cohen], 1939.
5. *Globe and Mail,* February 2, 1939.
6. C.E. Silcox, "Canadian Post-Mortem on Refugees." An Address Delivered in Convocation Hall, University of Toronto, March 21, 1939 (n.p., n.d.).
7. C.J.C., [O. Cohen], Report 1939, *supra.*
8. *Ibid.; Montreal Standard,* May 25, 1940.
9. C.J.C., Arcand to W. Crane, April 19, 1939. Photostat.
10. *Ibid.,* Arcand to Crane, July 25, 1939. Photostat.
11. *Ibid.,* Arcand to Crane, August 3, 1939. Photostat.
12. *Ibid.,* Arcand to Crane, July 25, 1939. Photostat.
13. C.J.C., H.M. Caiserman to L. Fitch, January 20, 1939.
14. P.A.C., Lapointe Papers, vol. 22, J.G. Drouin to Lapointe, May 22, 1939; *ibid.,* J. Matte, Secretary Federated Trades and Labour Council of Quebec and Levis, to Lapointe, May 25, 1939.
15. *Montreal Gazette,* July 31, August 4, 1939.
16. C.J.C., Arcand to W. Crane, August 3, 1939. Photostat.
17. F. Lefebvre, *The French-Canadian Press and the War* (Toronto, 1940), p.27. At the outbreak of war Arcand was replaced as editor of *L'Illustration Nouvelle.*
18. "I Belonged to Arcand's Party," *Montreal Standard,* June 8, 1938; C.J.C., Joint Public Relations Committee, Executive Secretary's Report, March 27, 1940.
19. F. Coté, "Fasciste d'un autre age: Adrien Arcand," *Le Magazine-Maclean* (May, 1961), 21.

Index

Aberhart, William, 43, 80, 81

Achat chez nous movement, 4, 7, 23, 33

Action Catholique de Jeunesse Canadienne (A.C.J.C.), 39

American Jewish Congress, 40

Anschluss, 113, 132

Appeasement, 101, 113, 128

Arcand, Adrien, 81, 96, 98, 111, 112, 113, 117, 118, 124, 142, 146; early career, 5, 7; joins Ménard, 5; forms *Ordre Patriotique des Goglus*, 6; and the Italian community, 7, 83; on the Jewish School Commission Act, 9; on the Bercovitch bill, 15, 21; his anti-semitism, 9, 11, 12, 18, 21, 22, 24, 30, 38, 107-08, 138, 143; connection with Bennett Conservatives, 10, 25, 29-30, 39, 42-44; connection with international fascists, 11, 12, 97, 146; on fascism, 30, 43, 144; admiration for Hitler, 20, 29, 37, 109, 115; promotes *achat chez nous* movement, 23; defendant in libel case, 24-26; distributes hate propaganda, 23, 24, 41-42, 91, 94, 128, 146; connection with German Nazi party, 27, 28, 38, 128, 146; opposes *Fédération des Clubs Ouvriers*, 36, 37; edits *Le Patriote*, 36; leader of National Social Christian Party, 38, 41, 44, 81, 88-89, 97; connection with Mosley, 88, 103-04, 107-08, 130, 142; on Social Credit, 43; association with western fascists, 41, 75, 111; association with Ontario fascists, 56, 95, 103-04, 112, 113, 114, 118; association with Union Nationale and Duplessis, 85-87, 93, 146; handles party dissidents, 88-89, 116; association with American fascists, 97; edits *L'Illustration Nouvelle*, 85, 86, 159; and Quebec Clergy, 115-16, 128; forms National Unity Party, 111, 119, 121-23, 142, 144, 145; opposes Paul Bouchard, 130; opposes Jewish refugees, 135; activities in the Laurentians, 143-44; activities in the Maritimes, 141-42, 145; personal characteris-

tics, 88, 97, 107, 114; policies,
88, 107-09; attitude to war,
125, 128-29, 130, 144; intern-
ment, 109, 145-46
Arcand, Yvonne (Mme.), 23, 130,
144
Arendt, Hannah, 3, 59
Auger, H.L., 86
Auslandorganisation, 63
Austria, 113, 125

Baldwin, Stanley, 101
Balfour Declaration, 12
Bartelotti, A., 84
Bayley, Charles, 7
Beaches Protective Association, 59-
60. *See also* Swastika Association
of Canada
Beamish, H.H., 97
Becker, Otto, 55-57
Bell, Leslie, 25
Bennett, R.B., 2, 9, 10, 25, 28, 29-30,
39, 42, 43, 44, 46, 75, 116-17,
126, 139
Bercovitch bill, the, 13-18, 21, 23,
24, 27, 40, 95
"Bert", 54-55, 152
Berthiaume, Eugène, 86
Blackshirts. See Mosley, Sir Oswald;
Fascisti; Canadian Union of
Fascists
Bland, Rev. Salem, 51
Blondin, Senator P-E., 25, 29-30, 39
Blueshirts, 41, 84, 90, 96, 104, 124,
129, 135, 136, 142. *See also* Na-
tional Social Christian Party
and National Unity Party
Bohle, Ernest, 63
Bott, Bernard, 73, 125
Bouchard, Paul, 130
Bouchard, T.D., 36, 88, 98
Bourassa, Henri, 14, 40, 131

Bourret, A., 110
Bracken, John, 70, 71
Brandel, Charles (alias C.B. Crate),
79, 81
Brandon University, 74
"Brassier, Jacques" (pseudonym,
Abbé Lionel Groulx), 32
British Empire Union of Fascists,
76-78. *See also* Canadian Union
of Fascists
British-Israel Federation, 141
British Union of Fascists, 76, 79,
104. *See also* Mosley, Sir Oswald
Britons, The, 12
Brownshirts. *See Fédération des Clubs
Ouvriers;* Canadian Nationalist
Party
Buck, Tim, 95, 103

Cahan, C.H., 64
Caiserman, H.M., 40, 94-95, 131
Calder, R.L., 93, 95-97, 122
Canadian Broadcasting Corporation
(C.B.C.), 128, 137
Canadian Citizenship Act (1947), 45
Canadian Club of Toronto, 46
Canadian Corps Association, 118,
119, 127, 134, 136, 137, 157
Canadian Jewish Congress, 37, 110,
131, 132, 134, 138; anti-
defamation activities, 40-41, 91,
94-95
Canadian Legion, 109, 119, 127
Canadian Manufacturing Associa-
tion, 109
Canadian Nationalist, The, 66, 68, 70,
74, 127
Canadian Nationalist Party, 45, 65-
71, 74, 75, 76, 83, 111, 119, 126,
127
Canadian Radio Broadcasting
Commission, 40